Culturally Proficient
Instruction

THIRD EDITION

Cultural Proficiency Titles

Cultural Proficiency: A Manual for School Leaders, 3rd ed., 2009

Culturally Proficient Instruction: A Guide for People Who Teach, 2nd ed., 2002

The Culturally Proficient School: An Implementation Guide for School Leaders, 2005

Culturally Proficient Coaching: Supporting Educators to Create Equitable Schools, 2007

Culturally Proficient Inquiry: A Lens for Identifying and Examining Educational Gaps, 2008

Culturally Proficient Leadership: The Personal Journey Begins Within, 2009

Culturally Proficient Learning Communities: Confronting Inequity Through Collaborative Curiosity, 2009

The Cultural Proficiency Journey: Moving Beyond Ethical Barriers Toward Profound School Change, 2010

Culturally Proficient Education: An Assets-Based Response to Conditions of Poverty, 2010

Culturally Proficient Collaboration: Use and Misuse of School Counselors, 2011

A Culturally Proficient Society Begins in School: Leadership for Equity, 2011

Kikanza J. Nuri-Robins   Delores B. Lindsey
Randall B. Lindsey   Raymond D. Terrell

Foreword by ALBERTO OCHOA

Culturally Proficient
Instruction

A Guide for People Who Teach

THIRD EDITION

CORWIN
A SAGE Company

CORWIN
A SAGE Company

FOR INFORMATION:

Corwin

A SAGE Company

2455 Teller Road

Thousand Oaks, California 91320

(800) 233-9936

Fax: (800) 417-2466

www.corwin.com

SAGE Ltd.

1 Oliver's Yard

55 City Road

London EC1Y 1SP

United Kingdom

SAGE India Pvt. Ltd.

B 1/I 1 Mohan Cooperative

Industrial Area

Mathura Road, New Delhi 110 044

India

SAGE Asia-Pacific Pte. Ltd.

33 Pekin Street #02-01

Far East Square

Singapore 048763

Acquisitions Editor: Dan Alpert

Associate Editor: Megan Bedell

Editorial Assistant: Sarah Bartlett

Production Editor: Amy Schroller

Copy Editor: Trey Thoelcke

Typesetter: C&M Digitals (P) Ltd.

Proofreader: Charlotte J. Waisner

Indexer: Judy Hunt

Cover Designer: Michael Dubowe

Permissions Editor: Karen Ehrmann

Printed in the United States of America

Library of Congress Cataloging-in-Publication Data

Culturally proficient instruction : a guide for people who teach / Kikanza J. Nuri-Robins . . . [et al.]. — 3rd ed.

p. cm.
Includes bibliographical references and index.

ISBN 978-1-4129-8814-8 (pbk.)

1. Multicultural education—United States. 2. Teaching—United States. I. Robins, Kikanza Nuri, 1950-

LC1099.3.C845 2012
370.117—dc23   2011039687

This book is printed on acid-free paper.

11 12 13 14 15 10 9 8 7 6 5 4 3 2 1

Contents

Forewords   vii

Introduction   xvii

Acknowledgments   xix

About the Authors   xxi

Building a Learning Community: How to Use This Book   xxiii

PART I. AN INTRODUCTION TO CULTURAL PROFICIENCY   1

1. What Is Cultural Proficiency?   2

2. The Case for Cultural Proficiency   19

3. Culturally Proficient Standards   25

PART II. THE TOOLS OF CULTURAL PROFICIENCY   39

4. The Guiding Principles   40

5. Barriers to Cultural Proficiency   58

6. The Cultural Proficiency Continuum   76

PART III. THE ESSENTIAL ELEMENTS   101

7. Assessing Culture   102

8. Valuing Diversity   116

9. Managing the Dynamics of Difference   131

10. Adapting to Diversity   144

11. Institutionalizing Cultural Knowledge   159

12. Your Action Plan   169

References and Recommended Reading   180

Index   185

Foreword to the Third Edition

As a child I quickly become aware of issues of race, cultural diversity, and equity in the early 1950s. I arrived in the United States in 1954 as a child when my immigrant Mexican parents settled in northeast Los Angeles, on the outskirts of East Los Angeles. My parents strongly impressed upon their seven children that we were all equal and had the right to receive equal access to education. In 1955, my parents moved near Ave. 43, close to Highland Park, a community that at that time was predominantly European American—the Ochoas integrated a segregated community. Placed in an elementary school that had no interventions for recently arrived immigrant children from other parts of the world, I, as a third grader, was given speech pathology for fifteen minutes a week.

Knowing how to read and write in Spanish enabled me to survive the lack of comprehensible instruction and the well-meaning teachers who constantly kept reminding me to speak English and not to associate with perceived gang members. I soon entered one of the most integrated middle schools (Nightingale Junior High) in the early 1960s with African American, Asian (multiple heritages), Latino (first, second, and third generation), and European Americans (low and middle income) placed at one school site and expected to get along. No cross-cultural education was provided, so lunch time was a living theater of survival and one of my best-lived cross-cultural experiences: learning to survive in a climate of cross-cultural tension and competition.

Upon completing junior high, I enrolled in Lincoln High School, the first school in the Los Angeles Unified School District to have student walkouts in 1968. In the late 1960s and early 1970s, Mexican Americans and Chicanos across the states of the Southwest made their voices heard in a civil rights movement that would change the lives of youth forever. The walkouts were driven by Latino student concern for the quality of their education, the high death toll of Latinos in the Vietnam War, and the growing voice of the Chicano and Black Movements. I survived high school and received good grades, and with an emphasis in mathematics, but was never encouraged to apply to college. I did so because my older brother, Jose, had enrolled in college and the Vietnam War was in my face. I applied and was accepted, while always looking for jobs to pay tuition, books, and transportation. By my late teens I was clearly aware of discriminatory practices, lack of academic rigor in my schooling, and the lack of K–12 schooling opportunity to maintain my home language with a high level of academic proficiency.

In the late 1960s, I continued to encounter racism, often harassed by police for being in the wrong communities late at night, and I became an active participant of the Chicano Movement. My drive to continue to further develop my skills and find ways to contribute to social policy, civil rights–oriented educational projects, and social initiatives led me to graduate from the university, obtain teaching credentials, receive a master's degree in special education, and complete my doctorate in education with an emphasis on community development and nonformal education. My persistent passion for educational access over the past thirty-five years also led me to direct national, state, and local projects and research grants that have focused on equity of opportunity, language policy, community development, and professional development of biliteracy teachers—guided by respect of voice, representation, dignity, and opportunity to reclaim historical, cultural, and academic presence. This will persist until my last breath on earth.

Reflecting on my past thirty-five years of work in ethnically and linguistically diverse school communities, what do I see as the most challenging issues that we in the educational profession must address? First the changing demographics of our culturally diverse nation and world; second, the existing achievement gap that negatively impacts culturally and linguistically diverse (CLD) low-income students; and third the need for transforming our schools for democratic schooling. Culturally proficient instruction is a means to that goal.

CULTURALLY DIVERSE SCHOOL COMMUNITIES

Under the first challenge, the changing demographics, I have witnessed radical shifts in the size and composition of the school-age population of our urban cities. An overwhelming proportion of low-income Latino and Hispanic, Asian (Chinese, Filipinos, Indians, Japanese, Koreans, Vietnamese, Laotian, Cambodian, and others) and English language learners are among the fastest-growing and lowest-achieving subpopulation of students in our nation (Baker, 2011). The demographic changes in our nation's schools, most notably the growth of CLD students, require the attention of all education stakeholders. By 2050, the United States will no longer be a majority white nation—with significant implications for our economics, our politics, and our culture (Kunzig, 2011). While the demographics of our nation are changing, attitudes resulting in unequal access remain constant. CLD and low-income people on a daily basis face microaggressions in many forms. As this happens across the country, some educators dare to work collectively to actualize the concept of equal opportunity—legally, culturally, economically, socially, and politically through culturally proficient instruction.

ACHIEVEMENT GAP

Currently, low-income Latino/Hispanic and Asian students and English language learners in our largest urban cities are not acquiring the high level of academic skills necessary to access a quality education. Student preparedness to enter the workforce is quite disparate among various segments of the nation's population. Considerable attention has been called to the problem, but the enormous white and Latino/Hispanic and African American achievement gaps persist and do not appear to be narrowing (U.S. Department of Education, 2009). Most alarming are the dropout rates, ranging from 22 percent to 50 percent in many parts of our nation, and the lowest enrollments in higher education among CLD students (Frankenberg & Orfield, 2006).

Imperative is the preparation of our youth who must be culturally competent to live in a culturally diverse and complex world of diverse values, cultural behaviors, and lifestyle priorities. This can only occur with culturally proficient educators. As a nation, we must develop solutions to effectively deal with the underachievement of CLD low-income students. A vibrant CLD population and economy demands a democratically flexible school system that is respectful and nurturing of its CLD participants. A culturally proficient and democratically based school system must seek to provide an academically rigorous curriculum based on the skills (reasoning, problem-solving skills, multilingualism, cross-cultural competence, computational skill, and understanding of our ever-changing science and technologies) needed to enter the careers of a global economy. Moreover, we need to ensure that education professionals perceive CLD students as a resource as opposed to a problem.

As we walk the path of the second decade of the twenty-first century, we must transform our schools from undemocratic practices that yield inequality to culturally proficient school practices where equal encouragement prevails. This implies that CLD students are included equally in the school and classroom as competent participants and learners; where all are provided the knowledge and skills needed to solve big and small problems; and all are equally prepared to be informed and skilled democratic citizens (Pearl & Knight, 1999). You can begin the journey toward the goal of a social democracy with the insights and activities provided in this book.

DEMOCRATIC SCHOOLING

In his book *The Audacity of Hope,* President Obama (2006) reminds us of an evolving U.S. Constitution, that despite its original acceptance of slavery, its core ideas of equal protection under the law, the right to due process, and equal citizenship under law have transformed our nation. Yet:

> [R]acism, nativism sentiments have repeatedly undermined these ideals; the powerful and the privileged have often exploited or stirred prejudice to further their own end. But in the hands of reformers, from Tubman to Douglas

to Chavez to King, these ideals of equality have gradually shaped how we understand ourselves and allowed us to form a multicultural nation the likes of which exits nowhere else on earth. (p. 232)

Since the Supreme Court decision of *Brown v. Board of Education* (1954) that over-turned the *Plessy v. Ferguson* (1896) decision of the separate but equal doctrine, as a nation we have entertained building a democratic pedagogy that seeks to provide equal access and benefits to all children in our nation. Among the guiding principles of this democratic pedagogy is developing critical consciousness that works to improve a more just, fair, and collaborative nation and world. In pursuit of these ideals, since the 1960s, an important question has been asked: Why were the public schools failing poor CLD students in a democratic society?

Paolo Freire (1970) says:

A democratic education equips students to engage in action and reflection . . . upon their world in order to transform it. . . . the students—no longer docile listeners—are now critical co-investigators in dialogue with the teacher." (pp. 66, 68)

CONCLUSION

If the nation is to respond to the economic, social, and political challenges of the twenty-first century, confronting and resolving the issues of race, prejudice, social inequality, and the underachievement of our youth will be essential to the overall national educational success in the coming decades. One important action that can quickly be acted upon is the special attention needed to eliminate deficit thinking. A teacher or administrator who believes a student cannot learn, for whatever reason, will not be much of a teacher or administrator. This book is of critical importance, as it delineates a process to achieve democratic school communities and culturally pro-ficient schools, with a focus on investing in the support and development of all children and youth.

Democratic schooling and developing our social consciousness begins with social justice. In dreaming of a world that is less discriminatory, more just, less dehu-manizing and more humane, the wisdom of Carlos Fuentes (1992) reminds us that:

[P]eople and their cultures perish in isolation, but they are born and reborn in contact with other men and woman, with men and women of another culture, another creed, and another race. If we do not recognize our human-ity in others, we shall not recognize it in ourselves. (p. 245)

Thus, as a community we must be cognizant that the nature of the conversation concerning segregation, integration, equal education, and cross cultural competence will differ depending on the particular sociopolitical context and history of each of our CLD communities. We must truly believe that all groups will benefit by participating in and contributing to the evolving conversation of a deliberate and strong democracy guided by democratic schooling—to raise our consciousness and cross-cultural competence.

We also need to question our nation's commitment to reexamine the values of social justice and democratic schooling, and their implications for the social, economic, political, and educational institutions of our society. This reexamination of values must encourage a renaissance of social justice in our country as we press forward to actualize equality, freedom, and democratic principles. In a world in which more than 80 percent of the people are non-Christian, speak a language other than English, and are not European American, our nation is truly a minority nation.

The book you are about to read will take you on a journey of democratic engagement, of reflection and action, requiring honesty and an open heart and mind. Engagement in its activities will provide strength to create school communities where dialogue, reflection, and action can be linked to educational practice and transformative change. In the process we have to be "patiently impatient" to see our dreams of a more just and humane nation and world become reality.

Alberto M. Ochoa, Professor Emeritus
San Diego State University

Foreword to the Second Edition

In the context of declining resources, increasing accountability, and the rapidly changing faces of our students, the American education system is called upon to address a vast array of complex challenges. As we struggle to meet these demands school leaders and teachers are seeking a renewed sense of instructional leadership—one that demands success for *every* student.

The second edition of *Culturally Proficient Instruction: A Guide for People Who Teach* helps educators understand that profound and productive engagement with *all* learners is fundamental to successful teaching and learning. Based on a pedagogy of social justice and inclusiveness, the culturally proficient educator instructs in a manner that builds understanding of the teacher's and the learner's world that engenders a value for diversity. This creates hope.

Access, standards-based teaching, assessment of learning, high-quality teaching, and accountability are all vital preconditions to improving learning systems. But each of these elements seems insufficient without a sharp focus on the cultural context and skill demonstrated in culturally competent practice. It is no longer good enough to portray high average scores—to mask a glaring fact that our system is not working for many of our students. A significant change is needed, one that embraces social justice and equity and also one where leadership makes clear that a culture of low expectations for *some* students is unacceptable.

The Oregon Department of Education's, *State Action for Education Leadership Project,* a statewide initiative to support education leadership development, is currently addressing culturally proficient practice in the context of instructional leadership. Across Oregon, state agency partners, association stakeholder groups, public and private colleges and universities, and schools and districts are enhancing our collective practice to become a more culturally proficient education system. From state policy to classroom practice, Oregon is taking bold steps to hold ourselves accountable for every student.

Our collective question stems from a need to know how we can best redesign instructional leadership to demonstrate culturally proficient practice across the system. Our theory of action is simply that we must foster culturally proficient teachers and leaders who are able to guide our educational system and workforce. To that end, coherent policy and support for proven practices are needed to accomplish two goals: (1) successfully teach *all* students with whom we have not been successful, and (2) provide favorable district and state policy scaffolding to support those who teach. This deeply important commitment is grounded in system accountability and represents an urgent moral imperative.

In *Culturally Proficient Instruction: A Guide for People Who Teach,* the authors gently invite the reader to question assumptions and perspectives that underlie contextual features of the educative experience. Authentic stories guide teachers through a professional journey into reflective practice while practical ideas suggest possible learning futures. Thoughtfully, readers are guided to replace well-intentioned, but culturally naïve practice with strategies that demonstrate skill and increasing proficiency. While the process of becoming more culturally proficient is never done, it is my personal and professional judgment that collaborative work in cultural competence and proficiency has helped to move our state system in ways not seen before. For this reason, there is hope.

Rob Larson, EdD
Lake Oswego, Oregon

Foreword to the First Edition

Those whose professional calling involves shaping the lives of children stand at an interesting precipice, one in which the national conversation on reversing low performance in schools, decreasing the achievement gap, and ensuring that no child is left behind forms a new and challenging vista. This book both accepts the challenge and brings clarity and direction to the task. Its significance is not only that it orients us to a new literacy, but it also begins to answer the call for specific strategies for teaching all children. *Culturally Proficient Instruction: A Guide for People Who Teach* enables educators to act on the proposition that all children can learn and suggests knowable ways by which to achieve the goal.

The authors have gone to a great length to provide a set of conversations at ground-zero level. These conversations are instructive, rich, and reality based. At each turn of the page, the book mirrors tensions similar to those in public schools across America where demographic shifts have resulted in increasing numbers of children on playgrounds and in classrooms whose first language is not English; who are poor, African American, or Latino; or who exist in an underserved population. The strategies are not canned products. Rather, they derive from the constancy of dialogue between and among teachers and administrators whose courage and appetite for understanding the relationship between learning and culture compels them to think differently about teaching. This book gives a context and voice to the notion that culturally proficient instructors add value and dignity to children's lives and a dimension of professionalism to their artistry as teachers and leaders.

Reshaping the culture of the institution is a focus where the authors are equally generous in thought. Here, they shed light on the complex transformation of teachers, leaders, and ultimately, the culture of schools. In so doing, an inherent challenge is issued to the reader to think differently about how culture is the stage on which teaching and learning is performed. Culturally proficient language and behaviors of teachers produce a context of human caring, high expectations, and a diversity of instructional methods by which to teach all children. Such behaviors go far beyond the notion that teaching is solely about content and discipline. Indeed, this book is about relationships. It is about ways in which Cultural Proficiency is a bridge to cognition—an unrehearsed powerful set of lines between educators and their richly diverse audience of students.

In *Culturally Proficient Instruction: A Guide for People Who Teach*, the story line holds true through the vignettes, the research, and the new practice. That is to say, culturally proficient instruction is a skill requisite for leaving no child behind. It is a core assumption, a habit of thought, a natural strategy in the repertoire of teachers and leaders working to educate all children. This book offers insight into the world of privilege in a world of despair and what can be done to close or eliminate the gap.

Educational research has for many years attempted to explain the relationship between teaching and learning and leadership and learning. The real question is, toward what end? My sense is that this book sheds some light on other domains where adequacy and proficiency will be needed for a new social order. These domains go far beyond academic work and test taking. In fact, the book suggests that culturally proficient instruction is a form of professional literacy for all educators. I applaud this work enthusiastically. It helps all of us to climb out of the doldrums over how difficult it is to educate all children to a twenty-first century standard of living and knowing. It raises professional development, teaching, training, and leadership support to a new level of importance. It is hopeful. It avoids hand-wringing while providing pathways to a more culturally literate learning community. Perhaps most important, this book punctuates the need for conversations about race, class, and gender and the enormous implications that such conversations have on how we teach, who we teach, and toward what end.

Ron Edmonds created a new moral standard for schools by proclaiming, "All children can learn." He left it to others to reengineer school systems, to rethink classroom teaching strategies, professional preparation, behaviors, and attitudes of the adults to turn this notion into reality. *Culturally Proficient Instruction: A Guide for People Who Teach* pushes us up this moral hill, leaving behind no one whose courage, belief in children, and skill are brought into the classroom every day.

Rudolph F. Crew, EdD

Introduction

We are delighted that you have chosen our book as a means for enhancing your professional development. Whether you call yourself a professor, a trainer, or an instructor, it is important that you understand (1) who you are and what you think about yourself, and (2) who the learners are and what you think about them. In this book, we invite you to reflect on how you influence what goes on in your classroom and how you engage with your colleagues as a community of learners.

In our first book, *Cultural Proficiency: A Manual for School Leaders* (Lindsey, Nuri-Robins, & Terrell, 1999), we addressed educational leaders, suggesting that they could make significant changes in their schools and communities by integrating Cultural Proficiency into their core organizational values. In this book, we have expanded our audience. This book invites you to reflect on your craft and praxis as an instructor and to critically examine not only what you do but also the attitudes you bring to your work. We offer this book as your companion as you create a professional learning community with your colleagues.

In an environment where the amount of knowledge, the diversity of learners, and the varieties of learning contexts grow exponentially, we understand that professional development is essential. With this book we seek to add to the resources available to instructors to respond to this formidable task with hope, confidence, and excellence. In the second edition, we sought to share some of the nuances of Cultural Proficiency that we had learned, adding terms to the glossary, explaining more fully some of the ideas we present, and sharing what we have learned from you. We also addressed, more directly, the relationship of Cultural Proficiency to instructional standards.

In this third edition, we have again updated the case story and references, and shared with you our ever deepening understanding what it means to become a culturally proficient educator. We have changed some of the language in the definitions of Cultural Proficiency, and added a chart that serves as a conceptual framework—showing the relationship of the tools to one another (see Table 1.1). The previous chapter on culturally competent praxis has been incorporated into the principles chapter. That chapter has been expanded with discussions of the principles found in the second edition and by adding principles that were in the original monograph by Terry Cross (Cross, Bazron, Dennis, & Isaacs, 1989).

In Chapter 3, we updated our discussion of standards and standards-based education. In Chapter 5, we have expanded our discussion of barriers, adding Derald Wing Sue's concept of microaggressions and providing additional language that we have found helpful in distinguishing dominant cultural groups from others. In the past, the term *subcultures* was often used. We, as authors, found this term offensive, as did many of our clients. In this edition we speak of *dominant and oppressed, marginalized cultures*. You will find adaptations of the activities that were in the previous editions, and a few new ones as well. Additionally, as more and more people are writing about culture, and culturally responsive education, our references are updated to include the latest works in this field.

As you read this book, we want you to reflect on the way you teach, the instructional environment you create, and the way that learners respond to you and to one another. Personal reflection is one step in the process that will lead you to becoming a culturally proficient instructor. As such, you will continue to learn more about yourself and about how you affect learners. You also will develop skills for creating a culturally proficient learning community among your colleagues and for your students.

Acknowledgments

We remain grateful to Terry Cross, lead author of *Toward a Culturally Competent System of Care* (1989). His work continues to inspire ours.

Our editor, Dan Alpert, is an extraordinary human being. Thank you for shepherding us—once again. Neither the process nor the product would have been the same without you.

Our relationship with Corwin's president, Mike Soules, is new and promising. We deeply appreciate your support of our work and we are excited by your vision for the ever-expanding community of Cultural Proficiency practitioners.

Kikanza J. Nuri-Robins, Los Angeles, CA

Randall B. Lindsey, Escondido, CA

Delores B. Lindsey, Escondido, CA

Raymond D. Terrell, Woodlawn, OH

Publisher's Acknowledgments

Corwin gratefully acknowledges the contributions of the following reviewers:

Jeffrey S. Brooks,
Associate Professor of
Educational Leadership
and Policy Analysis
University of Missouri–Columbia
Columbia, MO

Amie Brown, 7th and 8th Grade
Gifted English Language Arts
Teacher
Pepperell Middle School

Floyd County Schools
Lindale, GA

Gabriel Lofton, District Equity
Director
Wayzata Public Schools
Wayzata, MN

Cookie Winburn, Instructional
Coach
Richland School District Two
Columbia, SC

About the Authors

Kikanza J. Nuri-Robins, MDiv, EdD, is an organizational development consultant. Kikanza has spent her career working with schools, churches, hospitals, and not-for-profit organizations helping them to become healthy, productive, diverse, and inclusive. She began her career teaching elementary school and secondary reading. She has taught social foundations for schools of education and has provided professional development in schools and districts throughout the United States. Kikanza surrounds herself with art and music in her Los Angeles home, where she enjoys the meditative art of sewing. (knr-info@earthlink.net)

Randall B. Lindsey, PhD, is Emeritus Professor, California State University, Los Angeles, and has a practice centered on educational consulting and issues related to equity and access. Prior to higher education faculty roles, Randy served as a junior and senior high school history teacher, a district office administrator for school desegregation, and executive director of a nonprofit corporation. All of Randy's experiences have been in working with diverse populations and his area of study is the behavior of white people in multicultural settings. It is his belief and experience that too often white people are observers of multicultural issues rather than personally involved with them. He works with colleagues to design and implement programs for and with schools, law enforcement agencies, and community-based organizations to provide access and achievement. Randy and his wife and frequent coauthor, Delores, are enjoying this phase of life as grandparents, as educators, and in support of just causes that extend the promises of democracy throughout society in authentic ways. (randallblindsey@gmail.com)

Delores B. Lindsey, PhD, is Associate Professor of Educational Administration at California State University, San Marcos. She has taught elementary to middle school and is a former school site and county office administrator. As a professor, Adaptive Schools Associate, and a Cognitive Coaching trainer, she serves schools, districts, and county offices as facilitator and coach. Delores's favorite role is that of "Mimi" to her grandchildren. She enjoys helping each one collect memorable items that they find while traveling together, and then to write stories for the items in the collection. (dblindsey@aol.com)

Raymond D. Terrell, EdD, retired as Special Assistant to the Dean for Diversity Initiatives in the School of Education and Allied Professions at Miami University in Oxford, Ohio. He has served as a secondary English teacher, elementary school principal, professor of educational administration, Dean of the School of Education at California State University, Los Angeles. He has more than forty years of professional experience with diversity and equity issues. Ray lives in Cincinnati, Ohio, with his wife Eloise, where they spoil their grandchild, Darren. (terrelr@muohio.edu)

All of the authors can be contacted through the website www.therobinsgroup.org.

Building a Learning Community: How to Use This Book

This book is for people who teach. You may be an instructor in a preK–12 classroom, a university, or a corporate training room. You may call yourself a professor, a trainer, an instructor, or a facilitator of professional development. Whatever your teaching context or your title, when presenting subject matter to your students, three factors crucially affect your instruction: (1) your understanding of who you are and what you think about yourself, (2) your understanding of who the learners are and what you think about them, and (3) the way in which the learners receive you and the subject matter you are presenting.

With this book, we invite you to reflect on how you influence what goes on in your classroom and how you engage with your colleagues as a community of learners. We invite you to reflect on your praxis as an instructor. We assume that you have mastered your subject matter, so now we offer you an opportunity to reflect on how and why you teach, how and why you create an environment for learning in your classroom, and how and why the learners in your classroom respond to you and to one another.

We have written this book for educators who are teaching. While our primary audience is for preK–12 teachers, we recognize, as the case story reflects, that teaching takes place in many different environments. It is our hope that this book will inform the praxis of all who teach. Teaching in the United States is a cross-cultural encounter, involving a multiplicity of ethnicities, worldviews, lifestyles, and learning styles. Given these complexities, instructors need to examine how they address issues of diversity and to develop strategies that will increase their effectiveness. The approach we offer in this book is Cultural Proficiency, which gives both instructors and learners the skills they need to learn how to work effectively with people who differ from them. *Cultural Proficiency* is the *policies and practices* of an organization or the *values and behaviors* of an individual that enable that agency or person to interact effectively in a diverse environment. Cultural Proficiency reflects the way an organization treats its employees, its clients, and its community.

This book is for those of you who want to reflect on how you practice your teaching craft. After reading this book and engaging in the activities we describe, you will have examined some of your basic assumptions about your craft, and perhaps, you will have committed yourself to culturally proficient instruction. This commitment calls on you to change yourself, as well as to influence change in the institutions where you practice. The call to Cultural Proficiency invites individuals and institutions to better serve the learners who enter their classrooms.

REFLECT

Are you aware of educational policies, practices, and procedures that demean individual learners or groups of learners? Do you have colleagues who either knowingly or unintentionally engage in practices that demean learners? Do you ever call these practices into question? Are you willing to confront either systems or individuals that dishonor your craft? Would you like to engage with colleagues in a process that will increase your awareness of diversity issues and your skills in addressing them? Write your responses here.

_____

_____

_____

_____

This book is designed to be used in a number of ways. First, it is a text for professional development that may take place in a university seminar room or with teachers' at a school. Second, it can be used with a small group of colleagues as a book study. And finally, it can be used with a large or small group as a workbook. Each chapter has activities integrated within the text and suggestions for continuing reflection and practice at the chapter's end.

A format that you might use, or customize, for your group could include the components shown in Table 1. The approximate time for this format is 90 to 190 minutes. If something significant or controversial arises, modify the agenda to accommodate the time necessary to process the issues.

The intention of this format is to build a learning community. This is an opportunity for colleagues to learn about themselves and one another in a supportive environment. Support does not necessarily mean agreement, but rather it means respect for a shared desire to learn, grow, and become a better educator. A learning

Table 1 Recommendation for Professional Development Session

10 minutes	**Check-in.** Allow participants to make necessary introductions and share a bit about their lives. For example, you might ask each person to briefly share the highs and lows of their day, or over the time that has passed since you last met. This allows you to acknowledge that life happens, gives you an insight into what is important in the life of your colleagues, and helps people to focus on the work at hand.
5 minutes	**Housekeeping.** Reaffirm the ending time. Make any necessary announcements. If you know that a group member is not going to be present, briefly share that with the other members. This reduces speculation and reinforces that absent members are missed.
2 minutes	**Learning Goals.** Have the designated leader indicate two or three outcomes that are desired for the work of the group.
3 minutes	**Summarize** the assigned reading.
10–25 minutes	Ask members what **ideas or questions** surfaced for them as they read. It may be very helpful if each member keeps a journal while reading the book to record their thoughts, feelings, and questions.
15–30 minutes	Share the results of any **homework** that was assigned.
30–90 minutes	Conduct one or two of the **activities** imbedded in the assigned reading. Allow adequate time to facilitate the learning experience and then to discuss it at length. Remember that the goal is not to complete an activity, but to learn something from an experience. The deepest learning will occur during the reflection upon the experience.
5 minutes	**Assignment.** Have the designated leader for the next session indicate the section of the book to be read next, as well as any activities that should be completed.
5 minutes	Return to the **learning goals** to summarize the session and to assess whether they have been met.
5 minutes	**Check-out.** Ask each member of the group to share what they are taking away from the session. This could be a thought, a question, knowledge that was affirmed, or a commitment to action.

community respects the need for and protects the confidentiality of the group. Members seek to understand one another rather than jumping to judgment. At the same time, group members will directly and gently correct, redirect, or inform one another as they work through misunderstandings, misinformation, and misinterpretation of the reading and the discussions.

Whether you study this book in a group or work alone, you may want to use a journal to record your reflections while you read and then as you try out new approaches. Your learning will take place not in the reading, but in the reflection upon your experiences and through your dialogue with fellow learners. While each session will have a designated leader or facilitator, all members of the group are fellow learners throughout the process. The members of your study group should be people whom you respect and whose work you seek to understand. They don't need to be people who agree with you on every issue. Diversity in perspectives and styles will be a catalyst for your own growth and understanding.

When selecting the members of your group, seek colleagues who will commit to both the process and the values that underlie them. A goal for reading together about culturally proficient instruction is to engage with one another in a culturally proficient manner.

WHAT DIFFERENCE DOES IT MAKE?

Many adults can still recall and recite in order their elementary school teachers or the teachers who most influenced their lives. Successful physicians, attorneys, scientists, writers, and artists often acknowledge instructors as important role models for them. Despite this anecdotal evidence, for many years we had little or no research to support the hypothesis that teachers and teaching make a difference in learner achievement.

Since the mid-1990s, researchers have documented that high-quality instruction influences the success of learners. The factor that correlates most highly with learner success is instructor qualification, including teacher education, experience, and expertise (Darling-Hammond & Ball, 1997). Parker Palmer (1998) has described this expertise as a "capacity for connectedness" (p. 11). He states that good instructors can weave a complex web of connections between themselves, their subject matter, and their students. Culturally proficient instructors express this high value for connectedness.

Culturally proficient instruction is a way of teaching in which instructors engage in practices that provide equitable outcomes for all learners. Although individual instructors can offer culturally proficient instruction wherever they may teach, they most ably and effectively do so within culturally proficient organizations. A *culturally proficient organization* provides and supports conditions that create continuous learning opportunities for its members.

In Susan Rosenholtz's (1991) study, she found that instructors revealed two strongly held reasons for their continuous learning: (1) to deal sensitively with different learners, situations, and settings, instructors need a variety of skills and strategies, and (2) instructors need to modify their methodology to match changing needs of the learners. The research of Linda Darling-Hammond and Deborah Ball (1997), Kati Haycock (1998), and Susan Rosenholtz (1991) has clear implications for culturally proficient instruction. Through culturally proficient instruction, instructors inquire about best practices and reflect on their behavior in response to the various needs of learners rather than simply repeating rote skills and preparing for tests.

We do not ask you to love each and every learner in your classroom. We do, however, suggest that you care about each and every learner. Furthermore, we believe that because you have chosen to teach and because you are seeking to be a culturally proficient instructor, you have already shown that you care. You care about what you teach, how you teach, and those you teach. By addressing the issues created by the diversity of your students, you are communicating to each learner that you care.

As you work through this book with your colleagues, we encourage you to show that you also care about your colleagues and your membership with them in a learning community. Refer to these suggestions often during your work together.

- Be open to new insights.
- Be willing to be surprised.
- Accept that you will not always be right.
- Understand that some of your closely held values may conflict with the values of Cultural Proficiency.
- Remember that the goal is not to read the book to complete it; the goal is to use the book to direct your thinking and your work as you engage in the life-long process of becoming culturally proficient.

To Barbara Latimer Brown and Grace Ishmael Robins

Part I

An Introduction to Cultural Proficiency

Before reading further

- Read the previous section: *How to Use this Book* on pages xxiii–xvii.
- Consider why you are reading and what you hope to gain from the experience.
- With your learning partners, discuss your options for engaging with the ideas in this book.

1 What Is Cultural Proficiency?

If identity and integrity are more fundamental to good teaching than technique—and if we want to grow as teachers—we must do something alien to academic culture: we must talk to each other about our inner lives—risky stuff in a profession that fears the personal and seeks safety in the technical, the distant, the abstract.

—Parker Palmer[1]

GET CENTERED

Take a moment and think about students who seem to be on the margins of your school and are not academically successful. Focus your attention on one or two of them. How do you describe their behavior or their attitude? How do you think they would describe your classroom or school? Take a few moments and record your responses in the space below.

_____

_____

_____

_____

As you think about what you have written, how do you react to what you have recalled or this invitation to think of your students in this way? If you want to stretch your thinking: are there faculty or staff at your school who are on the margins? Take a moment and add any comments to those you have written.

This book is designed to identify and support effective practices, to assist you to identify harmful practices, and to bring into play change processes that support your

---

[1]Sennett, p. 26.

professional development and impact your students constructively. Cultural Proficiency is democracy at its best. It is an approach to individual and organizational change comprised of four interrelated tools.

FOUR TOOLS

Cultural Proficiency can be described as:

- A way of being
- A mind-set
- A mental model
- A worldview
- A lens through which we view ourselves and others
- A lens through which we view our organizations and the communities they serve

Whichever metaphor resonates with you, Cultural Proficiency allows individuals and organizations to interact effectively with people who differ from them. It is a developmental approach for addressing opportunities and challenges that emerge in diverse environments. In 1989, Terry Cross, Executive Director of the National Indian Child Welfare Association, in Portland, Oregon, published a monograph that changed the manner in which we do our work. *Toward a Culturally Competent System of Care* provides several tools for addressing the responses to diversity that we have encountered in our work. Although Mr. Cross addressed the issues of difference in mental health care, his seminal work has been the basis of a major shift in responding to difference in preK–12 schools, universities, social service agencies, law enforcement agencies, and health care providers across the country. We are deeply indebted to Mr. Cross for his continuing work in the field of social services and his generosity in endorsing our work as we have applied his concepts to education and industry. Cultural Proficiency offers a model—a conceptual framework—for developing oneself and one's organization while seeking to address opportunities and challenges in our diverse communities and agencies.

We like this approach for several reasons:

- Cultural Proficiency is proactive.
- Cultural Proficiency provides tools that can be used in any setting, rather than techniques that are applicable in only one environment.
- Cultural Proficiency's focus is behavioral not emotional.
- Cultural Proficiency is applied to both organizational practices and individual behavior.

Most diversity programs explain the nature of diversity or the process of learning about or acquiring new cultures. Cultural Proficiency is an approach for responding to the environment shaped by its diversity. It is not an off-the-shelf program that an organization implements through training. It is not a series of mechanistic steps that everyone must follow. It is a model for shifting the culture of the organization—a model for individual transformation and organizational change. There are four tools for developing one's Cultural Proficiency.

- *The Guiding Principles*: Underlying, core values of the approach
- *The Continuum*: Language for describing individual values and behaviors and organizational policies and practices
- *The Barriers*: Caveats that assist in responding effectively to forces that undermine Cultural Proficiency
- *The Essential Elements*: Behavioral standards for measuring and planning for growth toward Cultural Proficiency

The Guiding Principles

These are the core values, the foundation on which the approach is built. The principles are guides for individual behavior and are the basis for organizational policies and practices.

- Culture is a predominant force in shaping values, behaviors, and institutions.
- People are served in varying degrees by the dominant culture.
- There is diversity within and between cultures, and both are important.
- Every group has unique, culturally defined needs that must be respected.
- People have personal identities and group identities. The dignity of individuals is not guaranteed unless the dignity of the group is also preserved.
- Marginalized populations have to be at least bicultural and this status creates a unique set of issues to which the system must be equipped to respond.
- The diverse thought patterns of cultural groups are equally valid and influence how problems are defined and solved.
- The absence of cultural competence anywhere is a threat to competent services everywhere.

The Continuum

The points along the Cultural Proficiency continuum indicate unique ways of interpreting and responding to difference:

- *Cultural Destructiveness*: Eliminating differences. Seeking to eliminate what differs or conflicts with the dominant group.
- *Cultural Incapacity*: Demeaning differences. Tolerating cultural differences without respect or acceptance of the validity of those differences.
- *Cultural Blindness*: Dismissing difference as inconsequential. Focusing on cultural similarities without acknowledging the significance of cultural differences to nondominant groups.

- *Cultural Precompetence*: Responding inadequately or inappropriately to differences. Understanding a need for change and committing to develop appropriate attitudes and skills for responding to differences.
- *Cultural Competence*: Engaging with differences using the essential elements as standards for interactions individually and organizationally.
- *Cultural Proficiency*: Esteeming and learning from differences as a lifelong practice. Recognizing that both the differences and similarities between cultures are important and learning from both.

The Barriers

Overcoming resistance to individual and organizational change involves recognizing and acknowledging barriers to Cultural Proficiency. It is the exceedingly rare person who denies racism and other forms of oppression have existed and persist today. Being able to discuss and explore such barriers provides a context for meaningful change.

- Unawareness of the Need to Adapt
- Resistance to Change
- Systems of Oppression and Privilege
- A Sense of Entitlement

Unawareness of the Need to Adapt

Many educators and schools struggle with change that involves issues of culture. For those who are resistant, change often is experienced as an outside force that deems current practices as deficient or defective. Whether accurate or not, an adversarial relationship exists between those seeking the change and those who resist it. In the final analysis, the most challenging culture to be changed is often that of the school and the educators in it, as they learn to educate students who, historically, have not been well-served by public schools.

Resistance to Change

Often educators declare their commitment to culturally proficient practices, but then balk when asked to make changes to their practices. Reading a book or adopting a set of values statements is only the beginning step to creating a culturally proficient environment. Interacting with colleagues in a professional learning community will result in invitations to change one's perceptions and one's practices; resistance is expected and natural. It becomes a barrier if it is not addressed.

Systemic Oppression and Privilege

The historical and current existence of racism, sexism, heterosexism, ableism, and classism is undeniable. Disparities based in legal separation and impediments to access are well documented and described as ill effects of such systems. The ability to understand oppression as a systemic issue apart from our personal behavior is important to one's development as a culturally proficient educator.

Systems of oppression have two effects: on those who are harmed and to those who benefit. Those harmed from systemic oppressions respond from an emotional connection as well as well informed of practices that impact them negatively.

A Sense of Entitlement

Many of those who benefit from historical and current practices often experience change as a loss. Not recognizing that they benefit from systems of oppression and privilege, they sometimes are resentful and display a sense of entitlement in their response to changes that will move them toward Cultural Proficiency. Oblivious to the negative effects of systemic oppression, they are often puzzled by or resentful of the reactions of those targeted by systemic oppression because they are unaware of their own privilege. However, whether one benefits knowingly or unknowingly is immaterial, the effect is the same. Being able and willing to recognize one's privilege and attitudes of entitlement is fundamental to confronting and changing systemic unfairness.

The Essential Elements

The essential elements of Cultural Proficiency provide the standards for individual behavior and organizational practices. The essential elements guide educators and organizations in the choice and application of culturally proficient practices.

- *Assess Culture*: Identify the cultures present in a system, including organizational cultures.
- *Value Diversity*: Demonstrate an appreciation for the differences among and between groups in policies and practices.
- *Manage the Dynamics of Difference*: Respond appropriately and effectively to the conflicts and issues that arise in a diverse environment.
- *Adapt to Diversity*: Change and adopt policies and practices to support both diversity and inclusion.
- *Institutionalize Cultural Knowledge*: Drive the changes into the organization so they are systemic and systematic.

THE LENS OF CULTURAL PROFICIENCY

As you progress through this book, you will notice our frequent reference to Cultural Proficiency being a "lens," a "mental model," or "a way of being." To guide your thinking, the table in Figure 1.1, shows the relationship among the tools and the contrasting lenses represented by the two sides of the continuum. Begin reading from the bottom of the table, in order to focus on two of the tools: barriers to Cultural

Figure 1.1 The Tools of Cultural Proficiency

The Essential Elements

Standards for Planning and Evaluating

- **Assess Culture:** Identify the cultural groups present in the system.
- **Value Diversity:** Develop an appreciation for the differences among and between groups.
- **Manage the Dynamics of Difference:** Learn to respond appropriately and effectively to the issues that arise in a diverse environment.
- **Adapt to Diversity:** Change and adopt new policies and practices that support diversity and inclusion.
- **Institutionalize Cultural Knowledge:** Drive the changes into the systems of the organization.

Cultural Proficiency Continuum

Change Mandated for Tolerance			Change Chosen for Transformation		
Destruction	**Incapacity**	**Blindness**	**Precompetence**	**Competence**	**Proficiency**
Eliminate differences.	*Demean differences.*	*Dismiss differences.*	*Respond inadequately to the dynamics of difference.*	*Engage with differences using the essential elements as standards.*	*Esteem and learn from differences as a lifelong practice.*
The elimination of other people's cultures	Belief in the superiority of one's culture and behavior that disempowers another's culture	Acting as if the cultural differences you see do not matter or not recognizing that there are differences among and between cultures	Awareness of the limitations of one's skills or an organization's practices when interacting with other cultural groups	Using the five essential elements of cultural proficiency as the standard for individual behavior and organizational practices	Knowing how to learn about and from individual and organizational culture; interacting effectively in a variety of cultural environments. Advocating for others

Reactive Behaviors, Shaped by the   *Proactive Behaviors, Shaped by the*

Barriers   **Principles**

Barriers	Principles
<ul><li>Unawareness of the need to adapt</li><li>Resistance to change</li><li>Systems of oppression and privilege</li><li>A sense of entitlement</li></ul>	<ul><li>Culture is a predominant force.</li><li>People are served in varying degrees by the dominant culture.</li><li>There is diversity within and between cultures.</li><li>Every group has unique culturally-defined needs.</li><li>People have personal identities and group identities.</li><li>Marginalized populations have to be at least bicultural.</li><li>Families, as defined by culture, are the primary systems of support.</li><li>The diverse thought patterns of cultural groups influence how problems are defined and solved.</li><li>The absence of cultural competence anywhere is a threat to competent services everywhere.</li></ul>

Proficiency and guiding principles of Cultural Proficiency. The significance of these tools is the former impedes change and the latter facilitates and fosters change.

Notice that the barriers inform cultural destructiveness, cultural incapacity, and cultural blindness. Systemic oppression and privilege and a sense of entitlement embody frames of mind and sets of values that inhibit cross-cultural effectiveness. In the same way, the guiding principles inform the other side of the continuum: cultural precompetence, cultural competence, and Cultural Proficiency. The values represented by the guiding principles are embedded in the essential elements of cultural competence and support a frame of mind, or mental model, to support being effective in cross-cultural interactions.

In our experience across a range of organizations, the most effective and productive approach to addressing cultural diversity within an organization is through use of the tools of Cultural Proficiency. By focusing on organizational *policies* and *practices*, or individual's *values* and *behaviors,* organizations or people are enabled to interact effectively in a culturally diverse environment. Too often we hear or utter comments found on the left side of the continuum such as, "Why can't *they* be like *us*?" or "I just teach my subject and don't need to know about *their* culture—that is the parents' responsibility." Leaders and educators welcome and create opportunities such as those reflected by these comments to better understand who we are as individuals working in communities that may be different from us, while learning how to interact positively with people who differ from us. In a culturally proficient school or organization, the organizational culture promotes change processes that value inclusiveness, institutionalizes processes for learning about differences, and responds appropriately to differences.

CULTURAL PROFICIENCY

A DYNAMIC APPROACH TO CHANGE

Cultural Proficiency is an inside-out approach, which focuses first on the insiders of the school or organization, encouraging them to reflect on their own individual understandings and values. It thereby relieves those identified as outsiders, the members of the excluded groups, from the responsibility of doing all the adapting. Cultural Proficiency as an approach to diversity surprises many people, who expect a diversity program to teach them about others. This inside-out approach acknowledges and validates the current values and feelings of people, encouraging change and challenging a sense of entitlement without threatening one's feelings of worth.

Cultural Proficiency honors individual culture while focusing on the organization's culture, which has a life force beyond the individuals within the school or organization. This focus removes the needs to place blame and to induce feelings of guilt. The approach involves all members of the community in determining how to align policies, practices, and procedures in order to achieve Cultural Proficiency. Because all stakeholders are deeply involved in the developmental process, a broader-based ownership, makes it easier for them to commit to change. This responds to the issues that emerge when diversity exists among leaders, educators, and learners at a systemic level.

Building Cultural Proficiency requires informed and dedicated educators, committed and involved leaders, and time intentionally structured for relational development. Instructors cannot be sent to training for two days and be expected to return with solutions to all of the diversity issues in their school or organization. Cultural Proficiency as an approach does *not* involve the use of simple checklists for identifying culturally significant characteristics of individuals, which may be politically appropriate, but socially meaningless. The transformation to Cultural Proficiency requires time to think, reflect, decide, and act. These behaviors are all acts of change. The culturally proficient organization closes the door on tokenism and stops the revolving door through which highly competent, motivated people enter briefly and exit quickly because they have not been adequately integrated into the organization's culture. Culturally proficient leaders can confidently deliver programs and services, knowing that both instructors and learners genuinely want it and can readily receive it without having their cultural connections denied, offended, or threatened. Culturally proficient organizations also can be sure that their community perceives them as a positive, contributing force that substantively enhances the community and the organization's position in it.

ENGAGE

TELL YOUR STORY

The following terms describe how a person may experience particular social encounters. Read each word and its description, and then tell about a time when you experienced each particular social phenomenon. After describing your experience, record the emotions that reflect the experience at the time it happened. You may not have experienced all of the terms, so you may want to complete this activity in a group. As your colleagues tell their stories, notice the emotions associated with each social phenomenon. If you engage with a group to discuss these terms, select the terms that you relate to and listen to your colleagues as they tell stories that illustrate the other terms. Record the emotional aspect of each of the stories.

Alienation: Feeling out of place, not fitting in, not belonging to any group.

Example: The only one of a certain ethnicity, sexual orientation, or gender in a group that may have antipathy toward that culture.

Describe a time when you or someone you know felt alienated.

_____

_____

What were your feelings (or your colleague's feelings) while in that situation?

_____

_____

Dissonance: Discord, disharmony, feeling out of sync, offbeat, out of tune with your surroundings.

Example: Attending a workshop titled "Achieve Your Full Teaching Potential," presuming it was for professional development and learning, but finding that it is a meeting to promote a multilevel marketing business that sells educational materials.
Describe a time when you or someone you know felt dissonance.

_____

_____

What were your feelings (or your colleague's feelings) while in that situation?

_____

_____

Marginality: Identifying with two groups but not fitting in either; being rejected by both groups and relegated to the margins.

Example: A biracial person who is rejected by both groups because she refuses to identify solely as one race or ethnicity as it would require her to reject the other.
Describe a time when you or someone you know felt marginalized.

_____

_____

What were your feelings (or your colleague's feelings) while in that situation?

_____

_____

Dualism: Being a part of two cultures and having to hide that fact from one of the cultural groups.

Example: A closeted gay person who works in a straight, homophobic world.
Describe a time when you or someone you know experienced dualism.

_____

_____

What were your feelings (or your colleague's feelings) while in that situation?

_____

_____

Negotiation for Acceptance: Having to justify being in a particular role or environment because other people question whether you deserve to be there.

Example: A Latina who is told that the only reason she got a particular position was through affirmative action, then having to prove that she can perform the responsibilities of the job.
    Describe a time when you or someone you know had to negotiate for acceptance.

_____

_____

What were your feelings (or your colleague's feelings) while in that situation?

_____

_____

Multicultural Affirmation: Belonging to two or more cultural groups, while members of the group know about and appreciate your membership in other groups.

Example: A conservative Jew, observant of Jewish law, and keeping kosher while working in an organization that is primarily Christian but whose members are both curious about and respectful of Jewish holidays and keeping kosher.
    Describe a time when you or someone you know experienced bicultural or multicultural affirmation.

_____

_____

What were your feelings (or your colleague's feelings) while in that situation?

_____

_____

Multicultural Transformation: Interacting with people from several different cultures over time, with all participants being changed for the better because of the experience.

Example: An attendee at a Brotherhood-Sisterhood camp for several weeks during the summer, where youths meet and develop relationships with other young people of different ethnicities, religions, and nationalities; they learn from one another and are changed dramatically by their experience; they leave camp with a broader understanding and appreciation of people who differ from them.

Describe a time when you or someone you know experienced multicultural transformation.

_____

_____

What were your feelings (or your colleague's feelings) while in that situation?

_____

_____

REFLECT

Notice how the stories you (or your colleagues) have been telling stir deeply felt emotions. Think back to the problem situation you described in the "Getting Centered" activity at the beginning of this chapter. Did you notice any similar feelings? Is it possible that the person who was causing the problem for you may have felt alienated, marginalized, or another negative social phenomenon? Did you hear many stories that told of bicultural affirmation or multicultural transformation? Imagine what it would be like if, in your classroom, you and your learners could create experiences of multicultural transformation—every time you taught.

_____

_____

_____

CULTURAL PROFICIENCY: OUR VISION OF MULTICULTURAL TRANSFORMATION

Through this book, we share with you how Cultural Proficiency guides our vision of multicultural transformation. We believe that transformation can occur if the educator—teacher, professor, staff developer, or trainer—engages in culturally proficient instruction. *Cultural Proficiency* is the combination of organizational policies and practices, or an individual's values and behavior, that enables the organization or the person to interact effectively in culturally diverse settings. Culturally proficient educators—and organizations—do not necessarily know all there is to know about every cultural group. They do, however, acquire the knowledge, skills, and attitudes that enable them to find out what they need to know, to learn that information, and to use it effectively.

CULTURE IS . . .

In describing Cultural Proficiency, we define the term *culture* very broadly. For us, culture is the set of common beliefs and practices that a person shares with a group. These beliefs and practices identify that person as part of the group, and they help other group members to recognize that person as one of them. Most individuals identify with one or two groups very strongly—this is their dominant culture. They also may identify in a lesser way with other cultural groups. Often, when the word *culture* is used, the listener (or reader) imagines an ethnic culture.

Ethnic cultures are groups of people who are united by ancestry, language, physiology, and history, as well as by their beliefs and practices. In addition to ethnic cultures, there are *corporate cultures*, the culture associated with a particular organization. In a corporate environment, each industry has its own distinctive culture (compare the automotive industry with the film industry), as does each particular business in that industry (compare GM with Ford). Within a given school, each of the various departments has its own culture. Think about the culture within an accounting department and contrast that with the research-and-development department's culture. Within a school district, the overarching culture of the district distinguishes it from other similar districts. In addition, individual schools have their own distinctive cultures, as do individual classrooms.

Clearly, all these groups and subgroups have much in common, but in many ways, these groups—and their group members—show significant distinctions. Consider the images evoked by these groups: Apple versus Microsoft, classified personnel versus certificated teachers, administrators versus faculty, engineers versus human resource personnel, Los Angeles, California versus Tupelo, Mississippi. These pairings reflect the cultural differences within a larger cultural group. Apple and Microsoft both provide operating systems for computers. Classified and certificated personnel both work in school districts. Administrators and faculty members are both found on preK–12 school districts and university campuses. Engineers and human resource personnel may work for the same school, but their approaches to the people and the work may be as different as Los Angeles is from Tupelo.

Yet someone who knows the culture of any of these groupings could tell who belonged and who didn't. Culture is about *groupness.* Cultural identity is what enables people to recognize where they belong. Across continents and across time, people have made fundamental distinctions between *them and us.* As people in the twenty-first century, we have retained this human tendency to want to distinguish us from them—our tribe from others—even when doing so hurts both them and us. A culturally proficient approach to instruction helps us to overcome this tendency by helping instructors see and manage differences in their classrooms.

ENGAGE

DEFINING TERMS RELATED TO CULTURAL PROFICIENCY

Read the definitions for these commonly used and misused terms. Reflect on each definition, comparing it with what you thought the definition was. Following each one, write about how the definition affirms, helps to clarify, or challenges your thinking.

Culture: Everything you believe and everything you do that identifies you as a member of a group and distinguishes you from members of other groups. You may belong to more than one cultural group. Cultures reflect the belief systems and behaviors informed by ethnicity, as well as by other sociological factors, such as gender, age, sexual orientation, and physical ability. Both individuals and organizations are defined by their cultures.

_____

_____

Equality: Equal treatment in the name of fairness. Treating all people alike without acknowledgement of differences in age, gender, language, or ability is considered by some to be fair. It is in fact culturally blind and often results in very unfair outcomes.

_____

_____

Equity: Recognizing that people are not the same, but deserve access to the same outcomes. Equitable programs may make accommodations for differences so that the outcomes are the same for all individuals. Women and men receive equitable, not equal treatment in regard to parental benefits at work.

_____

_____

Microaggressions: Hurtful or discriminatory behaviors and comments that are often treated as isolated or insignificant incidents. Perpetrators of microaggressions are often oblivious to the impact their behavior has on others. Because the behaviors and actions often are ignored, and usually repeated over time, microaggressions are egregious acts of social injustice. The dynamic of the oblivious behavior of the perpetrator versus the feelings of flagrancy on the target person contributes to major communications and conflict issues. Microaggressions correlate with the first four points of the continuum: cultural destructiveness, incapacity, blindness, and precompetence.

Tolerance: Enduring the presence of people who differ from you or ideas that conflict with yours. Tolerance is the first in a progression of steps that may lead to valuing diversity. Teaching tolerance is a more positive approach to diversity than is genocide or cultural destructiveness, but it is only the beginning of a process that moves toward valuing differences.

Diversity: The presence of people who differ from one another in an organization or group. The term refers to ethnicity, language, gender, age, ability, sexual orientation, and all other aspects of culture.

Politically Correct: Describes language or behavior that reflects sensitivity to the diversity of a group. People can *act as if* they are culturally proficient by using politically correct language. A culturally proficient person may be perceived as being politically correct, but in reality, that person is *culturally correct*.

Cultural Proficiency: The policies and practices of an organization or the values and behaviors of an individual that enable the organization or person to interact effectively in a culturally diverse environment. It is reflected in the way an organization treats its instructors, its learners, and its community. Cultural Proficiency is an inside-out approach to issues arising from diversity. It is a focus on learning about oneself and recognizing how one's culture and one's identity may affect others, not on learning about others.

Culturally Proficient Instruction: Learning about oneself in a cultural context and creating an environment in which educators and learners explore the cultural contexts for who they are and how they respond and relate to one another.

Reflection: A conversation with oneself to probe and understand one's values and behaviors.

Dialogue: A conversation with others seeking to know and understand others' values and behaviors.

Standards: A clearly defined skills and knowledge base that gives levels of quality and excellence that are measurable and attainable by all participants.

Achievement Gap: A discrepancy of access and academic success that exists among certain socioeconomic groups and ethnic castes in Canadian and U.S. schools. Discrepant scores are often described by educators and researchers as evidence of lack of resources for students in poverty, absence of rigorous instruction and curriculum for students of color, and lack of highly qualified teachers in low-performing schools.

Praxis: The integration of one's theory about a particular field with one's practice in that field. It includes critical reflection about *why* one does *what* one does, as well as conscious application of what one believes to what one does.

_____

_____

Practice: The day-to day-engagement in one's vocational activities from the perspective of a conscious, introspective professional.

_____

_____

ENGAGE

CULTURAL PERCEPTIONS

This learning strategy is a nonthreatening and interactive way to introduce the notion of embedded assumptions and stereotyping into personal and group learning (adapted from Lindsey, Nuri-Robins, & Terrell, 2009). It is also an effective introductory activity (often referred to as "ice breakers") that helps create the conditions for reflection and effective conversation to precede consideration of deeper issues, such as those that accompany discussions about race, ethnicity, gender, social class, sexual orientation, faith, or ableness.

The activity can be conducted by any two people and within any size group as long as participants pair up one-on-one. Invite participants to select as a partner someone that they don't know well, or who they would like to know better. The seven prompts listed below are the basis for the activity. For ease of beginning, ask one person to be Participant A and the other to be Participant B. Participant A gives his perception of how he believes Participant B would describe herself using the seven prompts below. Participant B sits stoically quiet while A is providing his assumptions as to how A might respond. Then participants switch roles and B shares perceptions of how she believes A would respond to the prompts. The activity takes about ten minutes and is accompanied by much laughter and high energy. You might coach participants to allow both persons to complete the activity before engaging in conversation about one another's responses.

The prompts:

- Country of Family Origin or Heritage
- Languages Spoken
- Interests or Hobbies
- Favorite Types of Movies

- TV Programs Preferred, If Any
- Type of Music Preferred
- Pets or Favorite Animals, If Any

Once participants have completed the activity, ask them to stay with their partners for a ten to fifteen minute group debriefing conversation. We find these questions helpful for providing meaning to the activity:

- What were your reactions to having the responsibility and opportunity to describe how your partner might answer the prompts?
- What were your reactions to sitting stoically and having another person describe their perception of your possible responses?
- Please share your experiences in learning about another person.
- Which assumptions were accurate? Which were not accurate?
- What insight does this give to the process of stereotyping?
- In what ways does this inform us of the stereotyping that may occur when we face new teachers, aides, students, and parents?
- In what ways are stereotypes helpful? How are they harmful?
- If the school is large, how are these perceptions enacted with people we rarely see?
- What was the most important thing you learned from this experience?
- How will you use this information?

GO DEEPER

For the next several days, take note of how people in your professional setting address issues of culture. Note their levels of comfort with conversation about culture and diversity. Pay attention to how people describe colleagues and learners who differ from them. Pay attention to how you describe those who differ from you. The words that you and your colleagues use will provide insight into your values in this area. After a few days, ask yourself: What am I learning about my colleagues, this organization, and myself?

_____

_____

_____

_____

2 The Case for Cultural Proficiency

Obviously a society to which stratification into separate classes would be fatal, must see to it that intellectual opportunities are accessible to all on equable and easy terms. A society marked off into classes need be specially attentive only to the education of its ruling elements. A society which is mobile, which is full of channels for the distribution of a change occurring anywhere, must see to it that its members are educated to personal initiative and adaptability.

—John Dewey[1]

GET CENTERED

How often do you tune into the local news station or read your local newspaper, the print or online versions? To what degree do local news events influence your work as an instructor? To what degree are you engaged with your school community?

_____

_____

_____

_____

This chapter introduces you to Maple View, the city where the people in our case study live. The stories we tell with these composite characters present situations for you to explore in your journey of becoming a culturally proficient instructor. Each character and each story is drawn from people we know. These instructors demonstrate

---

[1]Sennett, p. 23.

an array of teaching styles and experiences as they face day-to-day challenges and successes of the complex world of teaching and learning. The people we describe teach in a variety of settings—public and private, prestigious and notorious, from prekindergarten through postgraduate, and in boardrooms and classrooms, corporations and public service organizations, offices and training centers. These settings for instruction may differ, but the instructors' experiences are very similar. The stories they share apply to teaching in the broadest and deepest sense of the word. We introduce a major character and a portion of the case story early in each chapter.

Throughout this text, we are inconsistent in our use of personal address, both in the case that follows and in the stories from the case. When, as narrators, we refer to people in the case, after introducing them, we refer to the characters by their first names. When the characters are engaging with one another, the forms of address reflect the context of the exchange. For example, some colleagues address one another by their first names. Other colleagues are more formal and use Ms., Mr., or Dr., as appropriate. In some parts of the South and some communities of color, people with doctorates or people who are held in high esteem are always addressed by their titles. Also, when there is a generational difference in age between the speakers, the younger person, even if that person has greater rank in the organization, may address the older person using a title. As you read the case, notice these differences, and note the contexts. Sometimes, the simple use of titles or first names makes a significant difference in how a message is received. If, as an instructor, you are not sure which form of address to use, we recommend that you ask the learners in your classroom and their parents or significant others, how they prefer to be addressed.

NOTICING A PROBLEM

Alberto Hernandez, known as Al by his friends and family, took time to enjoy his second cup of coffee as he read the morning paper at the corner coffee shop. He skimmed the local news to see whether the open house announcement for Pine Hills High School was included in the community news section. As the new coordinator of the School Site Council at the school, Al monitored the school news in the local paper so he could be aware of issues that the Maple View District and the high school might need to address in a proactive way.

Al turned the pages quickly as he savored the last of his morning coffee. On each page, he saw advertisements and articles hailing the city as a great place to live. As a longtime resident of Maple View, Al knew that the city's reputation as a prosperous community was strongly supported by local business advertisements. The reputation was further enhanced in the Maple View section of the daily *Metropolitan Times.*

Al stopped turning the pages and looked quizzically at the headline on the editorial page: "The East Side Story Needs to Be Told." The editor of the *Times* was accusing Maple View's city council of keeping the East Side story from its new citizens on the affluent West Side. Astonished, Al continued to read. He focused on "Letters to the Editor." One citizen had written:

I've been a resident of Maple View for over 20 years. I have lived on the East Side until 5 years ago when I bought a home in Pine View Hills. I still do most of my shopping and banking on the East Side. All my family still live and go to church on the East Side. I'd like to think this is one city where we all get along very well.

Al tossed his empty cup in the trash and headed out the door, still pondering the concept of East Side/West Side, and wondering what the real story was. Like the letter to the editor writer, he had lived on the East Side for many years; but, most of his life he had lived on the West Side of town. Often, he and his wife shopped on the East Side of town because he felt "at home" there and could always find the best of family restaurants.

The next morning Al read two responses to the previous day's editorial. One letter spoke knowingly of the efforts by city officials to keep the East Side story out of public conversation. The other letter defended the city's efforts to present a unified front on all public issues. Two days later, another letter appeared.

Dear Editor,

I have a story to tell about our city. I have lived on the East Side of town since I was born. My parents don't talk much about how they are treated here because they are afraid they might lose their jobs at the local factory. We are farmers and live in the farmers' housing project at the end of the East Side stores. I feel the tension that exists. Nobody really talks about the "story" but people feel it. My children and I are treated the same way that my parents have been treated over the years. Everyone's usually nice and polite, but when we go to shop on the west side we don't feel like we belong. The thing that really bothers me is that our children are treated differently at school. My kids were put in special classes even before they had a chance to prove what they knew. The same thing happened to my brother's kids. Our kids can read. Although their first language is Spanish, they can speak English. I guess people think our homes are lit by candlelight, and we sing songs around a campfire. Just like other parents we read aloud to our children. We tell our family stories. We go to church. We pay our taxes. We work very hard. And we are the untold story of the East Side.

The letter was signed: *A proud child of the East Side.*

Al was putting the pieces together. Underneath the surface of a diverse and unified community image were real questions about equity. Was racism or bigotry or ignorance at work here? Were these questions being asked by well-meaning people who had the best interests of the community in mind? What did he really know about this community in which he had chosen to live, teach, and someday serve as an administrator. To help him sort through his own thoughts, Al decided to chronicle what he knew about Maple View.

GETTING TO KNOW MAPLE VIEW

Maple View is a small city located within a major metropolitan area. The city's population of 200,000 comprises mostly middle-income and working-class folks who live and work within the community. About 5 percent of Maple View residents are in the upper tax bracket and work in the top-paying management positions in the area's high-tech industries and corporations. About 30 percent of them are considered working poor and rely on government assistance for child care and health care for their families. For the most part, families in this community, regardless of income, send their children to the local public schools, shop at the area businesses, bank at the local banks and credit unions, seek health care at the community hospital and neighborhood clinics, and attend local churches, temples, and synagogues.

The Internet has made government services readily available to many Maple View residents. According to a recent newspaper survey, however, only 75 percent of Maple View residents have access to the Internet in their homes. The survey also indicated that 90 percent of the homes having personal computers and access to the Internet are located on the West Side of the city.

Area builders and leading real estate business owners perceive Maple View as a prosperous community partly because of the community's master plan development. However, the waiting list for low-rent public housing indicates a highly diverse economic environment. A major state highway divides the master-planned, affluent West Side from the downtown and middle- and low-income housing developments on the East Side. A large shopping mall opened five years ago to serve the upscale master-planned community. The downtown area on the East Side is served by mom-and-pop merchants, including a locally owned hardware store and a drugstore owned by the same family for three generations.

The large, 450-bed teaching hospital, University Medical Center (UMC) located at the north end of Maple View, serves the health and medical needs of all Maple View residents. UMC has served the community for more than twenty-five years. Two years ago, the chief administrative officer at the hospital spearheaded the development of a communitywide leadership project: Leadership Maple View. The project invites community participants to apply for a one-year term. Participants who are accepted for the project agree to serve with their colleagues on leadership teams in which they identify a specific community-based need and design a team response to that need. Participants receive extensive leadership training during their one year of service. The leadership projects are supported by corporate and federal grant funds. Projects that have been implemented by Maple View's leadership teams include improvements to the city park located adjacent to the city hall, construction of pedestrian walkways near the hospital and shopping areas, and construction of two large billboards placed at the entrances to the city. The city's leadership theme, Growing Our Own Leaders, was used as the focal point on the billboards: "Welcome to the City of Maple View: We Grow Leaders."

The hospital, community college, and school district employ professional staffs of instructors, human resource officers, and administrators, as well as food service, maintenance, and transportation personnel. In combination, these agencies employ the largest numbers of community residents. The recent economic downturn has left the local governments and the housing developments in a cutback mode. Unemployment is up and spending is down. Like most mid-size cities across the United States, Maple View is recovering slowly from the recession.

A small, corporate farming area provides vegetables for a nearby packing company. Both companies employ more than 200 migrant workers for the seasonal crops. The migrant workers live in corporate housing near the East Side farming area of Maple View. The demand for migrant workers is consistent with the current demand for produce. The second-generation migrant families continue to live in the East Side housing projects and to send their children to the same local school the parents had attended as children.

Even in the current economic slowdown, the chamber of commerce calls Maple View "a great place to live and work." *Parade* magazine recently listed it in the "Top 200 Small Cities in the Nation to Work and Raise a Family." The school district is in the top 15 percent in the statewide testing program. The publicity and recognition that the city has received, combined with master-planned housing, middle- and low-income housing, and outstanding future employment opportunities, have resulted in a projected annual population increase of 5 percent.

Maple View School District

The ethnic diversity of the city's population is reflected in the student population in the local school district. Of the 25,000 students in the public schools, 35 percent are European Americans; 30 percent are Hispanics from Central America, South America, and the Caribbean; 20 percent are Asian Americans (first- and second-generation families from Korea and the Philippines, and third- and fourth-generation families from China); 10 percent are African Americans; 3 percent are Native Americans; and 2 percent are Pacific Islanders. Twenty percent of the total student population is in special education programs, and 10 percent of the students are learning English as a second language. The district reports seven different primary languages are spoken by its students.

The local school district responded to the increased student population in the West Side area by building the new Pine Hills Elementary School for Grades preK through 5 and the new Pine View Middle School for students in Grades 6 through 8. Three years ago, the district opened the state-of-the-art Pine Hills High School on the West Side of the city. The old Maple View High School facility on the East Side of the city was converted to a community school for at-risk students, adult school students, and community recreation organizations. The school district maintains ownership of the property and has a joint-use partnership agreement with the city council. The downtown and East Side students continue to be served by the original Maple View Elementary School (Grades preK to 5) and Maple View Middle School (Grades 6 to 8) in the district.

The local school board, the superintendent, and other district office administrators have published a shared vision to serve all learners in the district with outstanding teachers, appropriate materials of instruction, and high standards for student performance. For several years the superintendent and the cabinet, along with school leadership teams, have made a districtwide commitment toward culturally proficient educational practices. This commitment has manifest itself through working with external consultants, site teams, and community members to examine policies and procedures and individual values and beliefs focused on equity and access for student achievement. The current superintendent has served the district for the past ten years and recently announced her retirement, effective at the end of the current school year. The question facing the district is: How might we sustain our growth toward Cultural Proficiency during this time of leadership transition? The school board and a search team are currently involved in seeking a replacement for the retiring superintendent.

Maple View School District employs 850 teachers. Only a few are depicted in this case story. Nonetheless, their stories offer a representative sampling of the kinds of issues that teachers face and of the kinds of experiences, approaches, and attitudes these teachers bring to the teaching and learning environment.

In the following chapters, various members of the school community are introduced through the case stories of the teachers and learners of Maple View. We encourage you to go beyond these stories, however, to apply the methods of culturally proficient instruction to your own teaching and learning environment. In these chapters, you'll find numerous opportunities to apply culturally proficient instruction to your own teaching. We encourage you to fully engage yourself with these exercises. Try out the ideas suggested and give yourself an opportunity to develop your own teaching tools. Once you've tried these ideas for yourself, then reflect and evaluate how well they suit your own individual teaching style. You may readily apply some of them to your current teaching and learning environment. You may need to adapt some others to suit your current situation, and you may find that still others apply less readily to your current situation, but you may be glad to know of them at some future time, when your situation changes.

As with anything in life, you'll find that the more fully you engage yourself with the text and with the suggested activities, the more you'll gain from the experience.

GO DEEPER

If you wrote a letter to the editor of your town's newspaper about your school—or instructional environment—and the community it serves, what would you say?

_____

_____

_____

_____

3 Culturally Proficient Standards

Any set of standards rich enough for a particular learner will contain items unnecessary for many, and any set designed realistically for all will, paradoxically, be inadequate for anyone considered individually.

—Nel Noddings[1]

GET CENTERED

What might be some examples of the alignment of your deeply held values with your behaviors as an instructor? Think about a time when you felt that your behavior as an instructor was out of sync with your values and beliefs. What did you do? What did you feel? What do you feel when your values and beliefs are well aligned with academic and performance standards? Take a few minutes and write your responses to these thinking questions.

_____

_____

_____

_____

_____

_____

[1]Sennett, p. 79.

A TIME OF TRANSITION

Education in the United States continues to undergo restructuring, reforming, redesigning, and reorganizing to better meet the needs of all learners. From the mid-1990s through the end of the first decade of the twenty-first century, the conversation about reform efforts among U.S. policy makers and educators has been focused on developing national standards for teaching new instructors. The ten principles that were developed in 1992 by the Interstate New Instructor Assessment and Support Consortium were referred to as the INTASC Model Core Standards (Armstrong, Henson, & Savage, 2005). Those standards led individual states to develop sets of standards for instructors, learners, and administrators. For example, in 2000 California lawmakers passed the Public Schools Accountability Act (PSAA) that identified performance levels for all learners based on grade-level assessments. Following course content standards and performance-based standards, California mandated (CCTC) California Professional Teaching Standards (CSTPs) for teachers and California Professional Standards for Education Administration (CPSELs) for administrators.

By the beginning of the twenty-first century, state and local policy makers had implemented legislation that led to long lists of grade-level and content standards that identified specific information required of learners as they moved through their schooling. The content standards were followed by performance standards that identified what learners should be able to do and at what degree of proficiency they should perform. Texas led the way with standards that required all learners be successful as measured by statewide, standardized testing. The Texas model for assessment became the template for other states to account for learner progress toward performance goals. In 2001, the federal government reauthorized the Elementary and Secondary Education Act of 1965 (ESEA) and named it the No Child Left Behind Act of 2001 (NCLB).

For the first time in the history of education in the United States, instructors and school administrators were being held accountable for learner achievement on the basis of standardized test data for each "identifiable" group of learners in the school and district. In other words, since 2001, U.S. schools must meet or exceed target goals established by state-approved levels for learner achievement inclusive of groups categorized by gender, race, ethnicity, language development, and socioeconomic status.

As the standards movement progressed to become political mandates, each state moved in the direction of having its own set of standards; therefore, spelling out what students were expected to learn varied from state to state. The call for "common core standards" across the United States in early 2009 became an effort to set a clear and consistent progression of K–12 standards that would prepare students for success in college and the work world. The goals of the common core standards were to articulate the same standards and prepare students using those same standards irrespective of where the students attended school.

The Council of Chief State School Officers and the National Governors Association Center for Best Practices (NGA Center) coordinated the state-led Common

Core State Standards (CCSS) initiative. California was one of forty-eight states that participated in this effort. The standards, developed by states in collaboration with one another, provide common expectations for what students are expected to learn. The final set of CCSS, released in June 2010, has been adopted by thirty-seven states, as of this writing (American Association of Colleges of Teacher Education, 2010).

To meet and exceed these learner achievement standards, by 2014 (No Child Left Behind, 2001) instructors must align the curriculum with content standards, identify instructional strategies that align with the standards, select materials of instruction that support all learners, and use assessment data to inform their teaching practices so that more learners than ever will achieve at levels higher than ever before. Achievement by all learners is the underlying assumption for standards-based education. However, for all learners to be successful, instructors must know and understand how learners learn and develop, how learners differ in their approaches to learning, and how to develop learning opportunities that are adapted to diverse learners. The culturally proficient instructor uses learners' diverse experiences, perspectives, and learning styles to create a teaching and learning environment that is respectful of each learner and encourages positive social interaction and active engagement in learning and self-motivation. Teachers must develop new approaches and acquire new skills while at the same time learn to connect with the students in their classrooms in new and different ways (Pappano, 2010; Wilmore, 2002). For some instructors these behaviors required a shift in thinking from the traditional "subject-based curriculum" approach to a learner-centered, standards-based approach (Armstrong et al., 2005; Voltz, Sims, & Nelson, 2010).

Although the national attention has been on standards-based instruction for well over a decade, all instructors and educational leaders have not embraced the shift from a traditional teaching approach to a standards-based instructional model. The traditional instructional model is alive and well because instructors tend to teach as they were taught. Figure 3.1 illustrates the typical, more traditional model for instructional design and planning. Topic, or unit-driven curriculum led the way in most linear lesson designs, followed by selections of activities, chapters, and instructional strategies. Finally, the instructor typically prepares or selects assessments to test the students' knowledge of the content within the selected unit or chapters. The assessments or tests are ways to determine student recall of the content or performance of the learning. The test results are shared with students and parents and often filed away for end-of-term student reports.

Figure 3.1 Linear Model for Instructional Planning

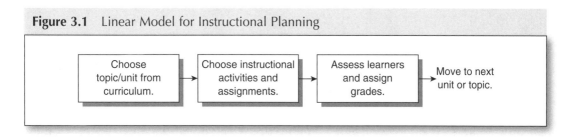

Today's complex classrooms require instructors to not only rethink their prior *mental model* for teaching, but to change their ways of determining learner outcomes, preparing lessons, selecting materials, presenting lessons, and assessing learner performance. Another way to explore the dynamics of standards-based instruction is to view the process as a dynamic cycle, as in Figure 3.2.

Figure 3.2 Standards-Based Model for Instructional Design

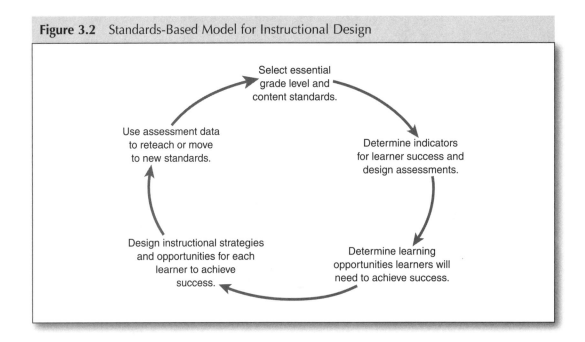

The teacher, often in collaboration with grade-level or content area team members, decides on the essential grade or content standard and determines the appropriate learner outcomes—what it is the instructors want the students to know and be able to do as a result of the teachers' instructional strategies and the materials they select. Then, the instructors identify "indicators of success" to gauge how they will know the students have succeeded as learners. Once they have determined how good is good enough and how they will assess student progress, the instructors plan their instructional strategies, select their materials and technologies, and prepare their complete lesson designs. Once again, these designs are completed as teams through inquiry and collaborative learning communities (Lindsey, Jungwirth, Pahl, & Lindsey, 2009). When the lessons are taught and formative assessments are applied, instructors review the assessment data and make decisions to reteach or move to new standards (Popham, 2008).

Figure 3.3 shows the comparison of key components of the transition from traditional, subject-based model to the learner-centered, standards-based model. The standards-based model begins with the instructor holding the learner outcomes in mind rather than a unit or chapter coverage-of-content as the teaching goal. An instructor or an administrator might monitor the learner by asking, "What are you learning today?" If the response is, "We are doing the questions in Chapter 3," then

Figure 3.3 Instructors in Transition

Traditional Practice (Subjects-Based)	Standards-Based Practice (Learner-Centered)
<ul><li>Select a **topic or unit** from the curriculum or textbooks.</li><li>Design instructional strategies around that **topic or unit.**</li><li>Design and give an assessment based on the information from the **topic.**</li><li>Give **unit** grade or feedback.</li><li>Move to next **topic.**</li></ul>	<ul><li>Select standards from among those **learners** need to know.</li><li>Design an assessment for **learners** to demonstrate knowledge or skill of those standards.</li><li>Decide what learning opportunities **learners** will need to be successful on the assessments.</li><li>Plan instructional strategies to assure that **each learner** has adequate opportunities to learn.</li><li>Use data from assessments to inform **learners** and parents and give feedback to instructor to inform decision to reteach, or move to next level.</li><li>Select next essential and developmental standards that build on **learners'** prior knowledge.</li></ul>

perhaps the instructor's outcomes are content-focused rather than learner-focused. If the student's response is, "We are learning how the economy of today compares to the economy of the early 1900s," then possibly the instructor had designed learner outcomes based on grade-level content standards.

Grant and Sleeter (2007) suggest that teachers be actively involved in designing assessments that draw from multiple and balanced sources of evidence rather than using a single source of data or test results. Collaborative teams of teachers working together to establish criteria, complex tasks, and multiple approaches provide diverse students opportunities for authentic responses to multiple assessments and performances.

REFLECT

Think about your instructional planning and designs. How do they compare with the illustrations in Figures 3.1 and 3.2? Has standards-based instruction influenced the way you assess your students? Why or why not?

_____

_____

_____

_____

_____

STANDARDS, NOT STANDARDIZATION

The accountability movement, fueled with the implementation of the No Child Left Behind Act, has school leaders and educators designing, developing, and implementing standards for learner achievement. To a large extent, the measure of whether learners have achieved standards is determined by standardized tests developed by states and aligned with outcomes indicated in NCLB. Often, the conversations in local school districts become arguments between proponents of *standards* and those of *standardization*. With high academic standards and levels of proficiency becoming the primary focus of instruction in today's classrooms, new questions surface about distribution of instructional resources, quality of instruction, and preparation of instructional leaders charged with the mandate that more learners than ever must achieve at levels higher than ever before. The urgency for learners of color and learners living in poverty is amplified in a North Central Regional Laboratory report (National Study Group of the Affirmative Development of Academic Ability, 2004) report:

> A comprehensive mission of public schools is to produce learners who are intellectually competent and prepared for postsecondary education and the increasingly competitive workforce. However, differences in educational outcomes of learners indicate that the impact of our current public school system is limited. One of the most urgent concerns among education stakeholders today is the underrepresentation of African Americans, Hispanics, and Native Americans among high-achieving learners. (p. v)

REFLECT

What do content and performance standards data reveal about your learners? Who is achieving at the standards level? Who is not? What conversations have you had with other instructors about the disparity in achievement scores of your learners? What thoughts or questions are surfacing for you as you read this chapter? What questions are arising for you about equity or equality in classrooms?

_____

_____

_____

_____

_____

Establishing standards and determining levels of academic proficiency do not guarantee that all learners will achieve those levels of success. Educators continue to search for ways to improve learner achievement. Mandates are not magic bullets. Data show that the largest portions of learners who are not achieving at higher levels are learners of color and learners living in poverty. The struggle for many learners to achieve these academic standards established by federal and state mandates continues in state courtrooms. The *Williams* case (*Williams v. State of California*, 2004) is one example of how learners of color and learners living in poverty must have their right to free and appropriate public education reinforced by the court system. The *Williams* case is not a case about how schools are funded; rather, it is a case about ensuring that all California learners have these fundamental tools: qualified instructors, a sufficient supply of materials and equipment, and safe and healthy school buildings (Oakes, 2004).

People who teach must be grounded in purpose, values, and beliefs that support all learners in achieving their best. This foundation is the *why* of teaching, and standards for achievement are the *what* of teaching. Successful instructors of all learners are clear about their answer to the question, "Why do I do what I do?"

REFLECT

Do you recall why you chose to teach? How do you renew and refresh to regain that purpose and commitment to your profession? In what ways are you serving students who need you the most?

_____

_____

_____

_____

COMPELLING DATA

Learner achievement data across the nation reveal the gaps that exist between white and Asian learners and learners of color, and between learners living in affluent neighborhoods and those living in low-income communities and in conditions of poverty (American Association of Colleges of Teacher Education, 2010; Education Trust, 2005; Hoy & Hoy, 2009; Johnson, 2002). Instructors are an important influence on learner achievement (Haycock, 1998; Marzano, Pickering, & Pollock, 2001, Perie, Moran, & Lutkus, 2005; Ravitch, 2010). In our work in schools, often we ask instructors to list the barriers to reaching learner achievement goals. The lists are long and include the learners themselves, their parents, their circumstances at home, their lack of motivation, their lack of time, their primary language, their culture, and even their friends. When asked, "How many of these perceived barriers do you have control, resources, or power to control or change?" the instructors often respond with various levels of frustration and describe their lack of control over such critical issues that influence the learning opportunities. However, instructors become highly engaged and hopeful when the conversation turns to the importance of creating optimal conditions for teaching and learning. Thompson (2007) in her study of teachers' and students' perceptions of low performances on state-wide tests, emphasized the role and opportunities of teachers and administrators to create an intentional, "no-fault" plan focused on culturally inclusive, well-aligned, standards-based lessons and assessments.

Effective teachers realize that culture influences their actions as well as the thoughts and behaviors of their students. To ignore the impact of one's culture is to ignore opportunities and challenges within the instructional teaching and learning environment. As noted by Voltz and colleagues (2010), the rich cultural diversity of classrooms provides teachers the following opportunities:

- Students learn languages, customs, and worldviews from other students;
- Students develop cross-cultural competence and open-mindedness to new and different ways of seeing, knowing, and doing;
- Students prepare for the global reality of their future work world.

The learner is the center of the teacher's world. A culturally proficient instructor knows and values the importance of standards-based instruction. The overarching goal of enhancing educational outcomes for all learners means *all* learners. Embracing student diversity, including all abilities and languages, requires teachers to hold high expectations for each and every student. High expectations are implicit in standards-based instruction and holds particular importance in culturally proficient educational practices (Voltz et al., 2010).

CULTURAL PROFICIENCY BEGINS IN THE CLASSROOM

The learner certainly influences the teaching process. That influence is described as the "inner curriculum" in the classroom. The underlying assumptions of the inner curriculum are summarized by Armstrong and colleagues (2005) as:

- Individual characteristics influence learning.
- Cultural identity is valued and included.
- Culture serves as a framework for sense-making.
- Learning is influenced by self-interpretation and self-directedness.
- Learners respond to individualization by instructor.

Cultural Proficiency is consistent with the learner-centered approach to standards-based instruction. However, we do not advocate that standardization be used as another way to sort and select learners or ways to reward the "lucky or already-equipped and weed out the poor performers" (Wiggins, as cited in Villa & Thousand, 2005). Today's classrooms are dynamic and complex environments for both learners and instructors. Often, school officials describe the "increase of diversity" or "the changing demographics in our community" as barriers or problems to overcome. Culturally proficient instructors view their diverse classrooms as *opportunities* to include and engage each learner in the teaching and learning experience. They recognize that it is *because* of our diversity that we are growing and improving. Instructors in culturally proficient schools acknowledge that the more diverse the learner population, the more opportunities there are for innovation, creativity, and growth. Sameness fosters sameness while diversity fosters growth (Barker, 2000).

Valuing the Hidden Curriculum

Culturally proficient instructors are aware of the power and potential of the inner curriculum for individual learners. Lessons are designed to value and respect the cultural identity of the learner and her or his family and friends. Classroom materials are selected that reflect the instructor's respect for the learner's primary language. Assessment tools and strategies are designed to reflect the learner's individual learning style. Culturally proficient instructors are constantly aware of the critical role that cultural identity and cultural perceptions play in the dynamics of the classroom environment.

The classroom environment itself is an influencing factor in how some learners learn. In addition to the inner curriculum and the adopted and approved standards-based curriculum, the *hidden curriculum* impacts the teaching and learning process (Armstrong et al., 2005). Aspects of the hidden curriculum include:

- School structure, climate, and culture influence learning
- Intended and unintended instructor behaviors
- Adults' behaviors that may differ from espoused values
- School structure that may not reflect all cultures

The hidden curriculum presents instructors with another opportunity to influence learner achievement through intentionality. Espousing that all children can learn by positing those words in a framed mission statement does not guarantee that learners will be respected and instructors will be trusted. Learners develop trust in instructors on the basis of the alignment between their actions and their words. High relational trust, as identified by Byrk and Schneider (2002), is developed through respect, competence, personal regard for others, and integrity. Learners are aware of the instructor's beliefs and values, not only by the words that the instructor uses, but also by the day-to-day interactions with the learner. The books on the shelves, the pictures in the room, the ways in which the chairs are arranged, and the proximity of instructor to learner are all opportunities for the instructor to intentionally communicate personal regard for the learner and establish rapport and build trust.

Instructors use multicultural resources to support their growth toward becoming a culturally proficient instructor. The twenty-first century classroom instructor must be willing to confront policies and practices that serve as barriers to culturally relevant practice. Often instructors feel powerless when faced with school schedules that track learners by ability grouping, traditional curriculum approaches, outdated textbooks and materials, limited or no professional development that supports multiple perspectives, and political hierarchies and relationships that prohibit inclusion and multicultural education. Instructors must search for resources, support, and opportunities to include subject area and content standards that focus on the diverse needs of learners, textbooks that include global perspectives and multicultural experiences, and instructor-led strategies that build communities within the classrooms. Professional development programs that include multicultural instructional strategies, selection of appropriate materials, and multiple assessment strategies support the instructors' efforts to grow and meet the diverse learner needs in today's complex classrooms (Banks, 1999; Johnson, 2002; Marzano et al., 2001; Nieto, 1999a; Reyes, Scribner, & Scribner, 1999; Villa & Thousand, 2005).

REFLECT

What factors in my classroom contribute to the hidden curriculum? How might I demonstrate my personal regard and trust for all learners in my classroom?

_____

_____

_____

_____

Cultural Proficiency Standards Are Informed by a Belief System

In today's standards-based educational system, several levels of standards documents have emerged. Elements of NCLB require states to develop content and performance standards for students, standards for highly qualified teachers, leadership standards, and institutional standards (e.g., National Council for Accreditation of Teacher Education, Interstate Leaders Licensure Consortium). In isolation, these standards are documents that provide guides and goals for educators. When combined with a belief system that values diversity, advocates for all learners, requires equity of resources, and builds support systems for effective teaching and learning, these standards become powerful resources for people who teach. The belief system that provides this foundation is one found in the five essential elements for Cultural Proficiency:

- Assess Culture
- Value diversity
- Manage the dnamics of difference
- Adapt to diversity
- Institutionalize cultural knowledge

Figure 3.4 displays the current standard-based context for schooling using the essential elements of Cultural Proficiency as a foundational belief system and standards of behavior for culturally proficient instruction. The essential elements provide

Figure 3.4 Foundational Standards for People Who Teach

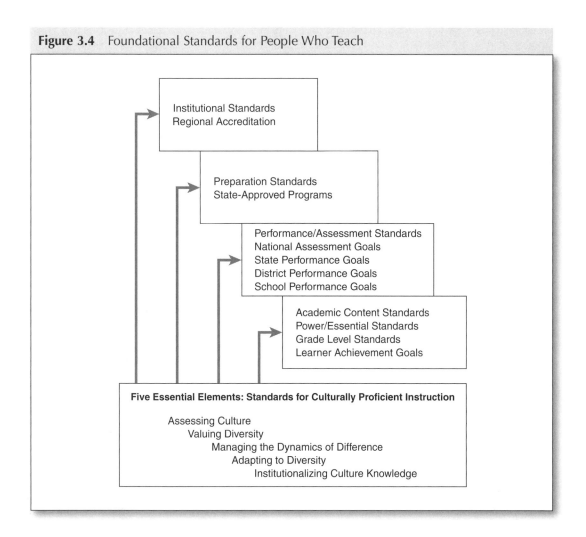

the foundation for classroom, school, state, regional, and national performance standards. Using Cultural Proficiency as a lens to examine assessment for learning and assessment of learning is one way to ensure high-quality instruction for all students, especially those who have historically not been well served or need to be served differently.

Figure 3.5 describes the culturally proficient instructor. The essential elements are the standards of achievement for the highly qualified instructor in today's diverse classrooms and boardrooms. The culturally proficient instructor establishes standards of achievement as learner goals rather than compliance requirements. Quality instruction is an issue of social justice and moral commitment to each learner. The instructor knows and values the cultural identity of the learner and uses that knowledge to provide a learning environment that is rigorous, appropriate, and safe.

Figure 3.5 The Culturally Proficient Instructor

Cultural Proficiency is the set of values and behaviors in an individual, or the set of policies and practices in an organization, that create the appropriate mind-set and approach to effectively responding to the issues caused by diversity. A culturally proficient organization interacts effectively with its employees, its clients, and its community. Culturally proficient people may not know all there is to know about others who are different from them, but they know how to take advantage of teachable moments, how to ask questions without offending, and how to create an environment that is welcoming to diversity and to change. There are five essential elements of Cultural Proficiency. As a culturally proficient instructor, you will:

1. **Assess culture.** You will be aware of your own culture and the effect it may have on the people in your classroom. You will learn about the culture of the organization and the cultures of the learners, and you will anticipate how they will interact, conflict with, and enhance one another.

2. **Value diversity.** You will welcome a diverse group of learners into your classroom and appreciate the challenges diversity brings. You will share this appreciation with the learners in your class, developing a community of learning with them.

3. **Manage the dynamics of difference.** You will recognize that conflict is a normal and natural part of life. You will develop skills to manage conflict in effective ways. You will also help the learners to understand that what appear to be clashes in personalities may in fact be conflicts in culture.

4. **Adapt to diversity.** You will commit to continuously learning what is necessary to deal with the issues caused by differences. You will enhance the substance and structure of the courses you teach so that all instruction is informed by the guiding principles of Cultural Proficiency.

5. **Institutionalize cultural knowledge.** You will work to influence the culture of your organization so that its policies and practices are informed by the guiding principles of Cultural Proficiency. You will also take advantage of teachable moments to share cultural knowledge about the instructors, their managers, the learners, and the communities from which they come. You will create opportunities for these groups to learn about one another and to engage in ways that honor who they are and challenge them to be better still.

GO DEEPER

How might I connect with the inner curriculum of my learners? What are ways that I might use the information about the learners' inner curriculum to design my assessment and instructional strategies? In what ways might Figures 3.4 and 3.5 inform my work as a teacher? As an instructional team member? How might the essential elements guide my actions as I grow in my practice?

_____

_____

_____

_____

What connections am I making between high standards of achievement and my role as a culturally proficient instructor? In what ways might I use assessment design and assessment data to adjust my instructional strategies?

_____

_____

_____

_____

Part II

The Tools of Cultural Proficiency

- The Guiding Principles
- The Barriers
- The Continuum
- The Essential Elements

4 The Guiding Principles

Before I stepped into my first classroom as a teacher, I thought teaching was mainly instruction, partly performing, certainly being in the front and at the center of classroom life. Later, with much chaos and some pain, I learned that this is the least of it—teaching includes a more splendorous range of actions. Teaching is instructing, advising, counseling, organizing, assessing, guiding, goading, showing, managing, modeling, coaching, disciplining, prodding, preaching, persuading, proselytizing, listening, interacting, nursing, and inspiring.

—Gloria Ladson-Billings[1]

GET CENTERED

It has been only a few years since preservice teachers were instructed to have a series of routines: "If you are talking, the students won't be, so always have something to say as you are moving around the room and especially when your back is turned to the class." Although much about classroom management has changed since then, teachers still do a lot of talking at their students. Students learn a lot about and from their teachers through these side comments and informal conversation.

How you teach, and the frame you create for why students must learn certain things, usually reflects your philosophy of teaching. During your preaching, persuading, and proselytizing moments in the classroom, what is the message you are

---

[1]Sennett (2004), p. 42.

delivering to your students? What is the intended message? What do you suppose they are really learning about who you are and what you believe?

_____

_____

_____

_____

Learner success depends on the quality of instruction, regardless of other variables that influence achievement. High-quality teaching relies on an environment that fosters the ongoing learning of the instructor. To guide you in creating an environment fostering culturally proficient instruction, we have designed a hypothetical case, drawn from our own experiences with instructors in a variety of settings, and which you were introduced to in Chapter 2. Buendia and his fellow researchers (2004) write about the importance of context when they speak of the *geography of differences*. We elaborate on this notion of geographical differences creating equity and inequity, access and nonaccess, to educational opportunities as the backdrop for the composite case story we present in this book.

This case introduces you to culturally proficient instruction, as it is developed and practiced within a community of instructors and learners. Throughout this book, various stories from the case illustrate aspects of culturally proficient instruction. Here is an example:

A few members of the Pine Hills High School accreditation team were curious about a phenomenon they discovered at the school. Some of the students, who otherwise were underperforming at this particular school, were performing at high levels in mathematics. The research team wanted to know what educational experiences these particular African American males had in common.

In time, they found that each of the young men had taken ninth-grade math with the same teacher, Ms. Brown. The research team was excited to interview Ms. Brown to learn more about the instructional strategies, the textbook, or the assessment strategies that she used to make this significant difference in the performance of her students. Ms. Brown was as surprised as the research team about these findings. When asked, "What do you do that is so different from what other teachers do?" she took only a few minutes to phrase her response: "I don't know what all the fuss is about. I teach the way I teach because I love each of them. Each child is special to me. *Why would I not teach each one?*"

WHAT DIFFERENCE DO YOU MAKE?

You probably already believe that you can make a difference with your students because you have personally experienced the way in which some instructors have made a difference in your life. Take a moment now to think about the instructors who have most influenced you. What did they say and do that made a difference to you? What do you know about their values? Before you read more about culturally proficient instruction, reflect on how these influential instructors taught, and then consider their teaching practices and the values you inferred from them.

REFLECT

After thinking about the best instructors you have had, list the teaching practices they employed. What did they do? What did they say? What happened in their classrooms? What happened during chance or out of the classroom encounters with them? Can you remember whether they reached out only to you, or did they do something that showed they noticed and valued each learner?

_____

_____

_____

_____

Perhaps your list included these elements:

- The instructors had mastered their subject matter and the craft of teaching, and they knew what they were doing.
- They cared that people learned.
- They created a space where it was safe to take the risks necessary for learning.
- They absolutely, unabashedly, loved what they were doing.
- They acknowledged the worldview of the learners and attempted to connect the learning experience to the context of the learner.
- They found a way to connect to each learner in a way that was meaningful to them.

These traits are commonly cited in conversations about influential teachers (Lindsey, 2000).

Karen Kent (1999) describes stages of teacher development that she has observed. In her schema, the two most advanced levels are the *experienced instructor*, who functions as a colleague, and the *accomplished instructor*, who functions as a professional. The experienced instructor asks, "What do my colleagues and I need to learn more about in order to improve our students' learning and performance?" (p. 16). The accomplished, professional instructor asks questions such as, "How does good teaching practice get infused into educational policy and influence those policies that affect the quality of teaching and learning in the classroom?" (p. 17).

Experienced instructors want to know how culture has shaped them and their students. Accomplished instructors seek to take this cultural knowledge and institutionalize it into new policies and practices. These new policies and practices often replace ones that had limited students' access to knowledge and success in classrooms and training rooms. Thus, culturally proficient instructors seek to learn not only about the students but also about themselves in a cultural context. They also seek to create an environment in which learners are invited to explore the cultural contexts for who they are and how they relate to one another.

This is most easily done within the framework of one's values. Values are non-negotiable beliefs about what is good, just, and beautiful. Your values are the lenses through which you view the world and interpret your experiences. When you reflect upon your values, you understand how they influence your perceptions and your behaviors. When you are mindful of your values, they become the guiding principles for your decisions and your actions.

REFLECT

What are your values about teaching, learning, and instructional environments? What are your values about culture and diversity?

_____

_____

_____

_____

THE GUIDING PRINCIPLES

The guiding principles of Cultural Proficiency are attitudinal benchmarks; they determine what you do and they shape how you do it. The principles are the values of Cultural Proficiency, and they serve as lenses for understanding classroom interactions and are guidelines for assessing how you engage with your colleagues, your students, and their communities.

- Culture is a predominant force in shaping values, behaviors, and institutions.
- People are served in varying degrees by the dominant culture.

- People who are not part of the dominant culture have to be at least bicultural.
- Marginalized populations have to be at least bicultural and this status creates a unique set of issues to which the system must be equipped to respond.
- There is diversity within and between cultures, and both are important.
- Every group has unique, culturally defined needs that must be respected.
- People have personal identities and group identities. The dignity of individuals is not guaranteed unless the dignity of the group is also preserved.
- The family, as defined by each culture, is the primary system of support in the education of children.
- The diverse thought patterns of cultural groups are equally valid and influence how problems are defined and solved.
- The absence of cultural competence anywhere is a threat to competent services everywhere.

REFLECT

After assessing your own values about culture, diversity, and inclusion, compare them to the guiding principles, or values, of Cultural Proficiency to determine what is missing in your perspectives.

Look at the statements that reflect the values of your school or district. They might be found in mission statements or values statements posted in the school or district offices. How do they compare to the guiding principles or values of Cultural Proficiency?

Have a conversation with your colleagues about the guiding principles. What makes sense to you? What don't you understand? What affirms your experience? What do you need to learn more about?

_____

_____

_____

_____

Culture is a predominant force in shaping values, behaviors, and institutions. Culture is about groupness, not just ethnicity. Culture is the set of shared beliefs and behaviors of any group that distinguishes the group members from others. Culture is not a problem to be solved; however, culture often determines what is perceived as a problem and what are acceptable approaches to solving the problem. You cannot *not* have a culture; if, however you do not notice your culture or the culture of your organization, it is probably because you are a member of the dominant culture. As an instructor, it is important to acknowledge culture as a predominant force in shaping behaviors, values, and institutions. Culture determines how you interact with your learners and react to things that happen in the classroom. Cultural biases invite you to judge behavior that differs from yours. Cultural differences are sometimes the cause of behaviors in others that you might find offensive. The organizational norms, the school climate, and the unwritten rules of your organization are all a reflection of its culture.

REFLECT

What is your culture? (Remember culture is more than race or ethnicity.) How has your culture shaped you? How might it bias you?

Identify some of the conflicts and congruencies between the culture of your school or organization and the culture of the learners that attend the school and the communities from which they come.

_____

_____

_____

_____

While reflecting on organizations in which you have worked, describe an organizational policy or practice that affirms this guiding principle.

Describe an instructional behavior of yours, or of someone you know, that illustrates this principle.

_____

_____

_____

_____

People are served in varying degrees by the dominant culture. When you know all of the rules—the official stated rules and the unofficial, unwritten rules—you have a better chance of being successful at the game. If you have had experience playing by the rules and most of the people in your home and community know and abide by the same set of rules as you do, you are at an advantage. You know what to expect and what is expected of you. On the other hand, if you don't know the rules of the place where you are, or how they differ from the rules in the place where you were, you will be at a disadvantage. The degree to which learners and their families successfully navigate the cultures of the school and the classroom is directly related to how well they know the cultural expectations of those environments.

If you are a member of the dominant culture, you may not even notice the many ways that the culture of your organization or group affects those who do not know the cultural norms or rules. What works for you in your classroom, your organization, and your community may work against members of other cultural groups. Often, when members of dominant cultures recognize that there are cultural differences, they suggest that the persons in nondominant (beta) cultures simply change and learn the new rules. In other situations, it is assumed that the beta groups do know the rules or ought to know them, and instead of being taught the new rules, the learners are punished for not knowing them. This approach puts the burden for change on just the beta groups. In a culturally proficient environment, rather than chastising group members for not knowing the rules, the cultural expectations are taught, explicitly, to everyone. A commitment to Cultural Proficiency is a commitment to a dynamic relationship in which all parties learn from one another and adapt as they adjust to their differences.

REFLECT

What works for the dominant culture of your organization or school that may not work for all its instructors or students?

_____

_____

_____

_____

While reflecting on organizations in which you have worked, describe an organizational policy or practice that affirms this guiding principle.

_____

_____

_____

_____

Describe an instructional behavior of yours or of someone you know that illustrates this principle.

_____

_____

_____

_____

People who are not part of the dominant culture have to be at least bicultural. Marginalized populations have to be at least bicultural and this status creates a unique set of issues to which the system must be equipped to respond. English language learners, immigrant students, students from families of extreme poverty or from marginalized ethnic groups, must know the norms, values, and cultural expectations of their native cultures in order to survive. They bring this knowledge to school. Once there, they must learn the cultural expectations of school and then figure out where there is conflict and congruence between the two sets of norms.

When we are part of the dominant culture, we often fail to recognize all that is required of members of beta cultures. As educators, regardless of our sexuality, gender, or ethnicity, we belong to the group of educators, and as educators, we are members of a dominant group. Educators establish the norms for schools and have the power to punish those who do not conform.

Schools are viewed and experienced in at least three different ways by our diverse parent/guardian populations. In the first group are parents who had positive experiences as students themselves, and for them school is familiar and friendly. The second group is comprised of parents who were not successful, or who slid through school mostly unnoticed by educators, and are much less likely to be excited to visit school and restimulate old hurts. A third group is parents from cultural groups that believe it intrusive to be involved in their children's school. In other words, the educators "know what is best for their child." To make life more interesting, it is very common to have all three of these types of parents and guardians in the same school, further complicating the work of teachers and administrators.

The culturally proficient educator recognizes that, to be successful, parents from the latter two groups have to be fluent in the communication patterns of the school, as well as the communication patterns that exist in their communities. The effective educator teaches the cultural norms and expectations of schools and is prepared for conflict when the norms and expectations are different from those in their communities, their countries of origin, or their cultural groups. Such educators support parents and guardians and their children in developing bicultural skills, learning to code-switch appropriately as the cultural expectations of their environments change.

REFLECT

What is it about your classroom or school that may be inviting to parents? What about your classroom or school may put off some of your parents?

_____

_____

_____

_____

_____

How do you know whether parents feel invited or put off? Try to be as candid as you can be.

_____

_____

_____

_____

_____

REFLECT

Think of a group to which you belong wherein you are not part of the dominant culture. What works for the dominant culture of that group and doesn't work for you?

_____

_____

_____

_____

What works for the dominant culture of your organization or school that may not work for all its instructors or students?

_____

_____

_____

_____

While reflecting on organizations in which you have worked, describe an organizational policy or practice that affirms this guiding principle.

_____

_____

_____

_____

Describe an instructional behavior of yours or of someone you know that illustrates this principle.

_____

_____

_____

_____

There is diversity within and between cultures, and both are important. Because diversity within cultures is as important as diversity among cultures, it is important to learn about cultural groups, not as monoliths—such as women, Asians, or gay people—but as the complex and diverse groups of individuals that they are. Some women identify first as women, others as members of their ethnic groups, and some by their sexual orientation. Women are educated, ignorant, professionals, and stay-at-home moms. As a category, the term *Asians* tells us what the group is not, and that is almost all it does. Which Asian group are we talking about? From India? China? Jordan? Second-generation immigrant or Japanese national? Sexual orientation is also very complicated as reflected in the names for the demographic groups within the gay community (e.g., lesbian, gay, bisexual, and transgendered). These groups are characterized by socioeconomic class, education, and gender as well.

In the United States, each of the major ethnic and cultural groups is divided along class lines. There are poor, working-class, middle-class, and upper-class people among all the groups. Economic class, education, and immigrant status all inform and shape one's culture. Stereotypes are short cuts that allow us to take advantage of prior experiences and past learning. However when stereotypes are used without testing them or gathering additional data, they become dysfunctional. Stereotypes about particular groups give the impression that all members of a group share the same characteristics as all other members of the group.

REFLECT

What are some of the groups within the major cultures represented in your organization? How might the differences within groups affect the way you deliver your instruction or other services?

_____

_____

_____

_____

While reflecting on organizations in which you have worked, describe an organizational policy or practice that affirms this guiding principle.

_____

_____

_____

_____

Describe an instructional behavior of yours, or of someone you know, that illustrates this principle.

_____

_____

_____

_____

Every group has unique, culturally defined needs that must be respected. You teach respect by showing respect in ways that are meaningful to the receiver. Because a culturally defined practice differs from yours doesn't make it wrong. It may however be inappropriate or impractical for a learning environment. Before communicating to learners and their families about what may and may not take place in your school or organization, ask yourself about the reasons for your objection. Each cultural group has unique needs that cannot be met within the boundaries of the dominant culture. Many, however, can. Make room in your organization for several paths leading to the same goal. Within your classroom, the concept of differentiated instruction invites you to plan for a variety of learning styles. When you develop a lesson, you consider that some learners need concrete examples; others are more comfortable with abstract ideas. Some learners respond to visual cues, whereas others must be physically engaged before they grasp a concept. People who teach, even if their teaching style favors one mode of learning over another, usually respect differences in how people learn new ideas. Differences in cultural needs also invite acknowledgment and respect from instructors.

REFLECT

What are some of the unique, culturally defined needs that are being acknowledged in your instructional environment?

Tell of a time when a student was targeted (i.e., attacked or made the object of derision) for seeking to have a culturally defined need met at school or in your organization.

_____

_____

_____

_____

While reflecting on organizations in which you have worked, describe an organizational policy or practice that affirms this guiding principle.

_____

_____

_____

_____

Describe an instructional behavior of yours or of someone you know that illustrates this principle.

_____

_____

_____

_____

People have personal identities and group identities. The dignity of individuals is not guaranteed unless the dignity of the group is also preserved. Although it is important to treat all people as individuals, it is also important to acknowledge that individuals have group identities as well. Making negative comments or reinforcing a negative stereotype about the group is insulting to its members. Moreover, attempting to separate the person from her or his group by telling the person, "You're different; you're not like those other Xs," is offensive and denies that the person may identify strongly with other Xs. These actions are called *microaggressions*—small actions or statements that target an individual or the group to which the individual belongs (see Sue, 2010). Microaggressions are insidious because they can easily be dismissed as inconsequential, or the targeted person can be dismissed as overly sensitive. Yet, microaggressions tend to come in clusters. As unwanted and repeated behaviors, they undermine the work of the best instructors and derail the work of less competent ones.

REFLECT

List some words and phrases that might insult or discount members of cultural groups in your organization.

_____

_____

_____

_____

Tell how you have been targeted by microaggressions because of groups you are perceived to represent. Tell of a time you sought to be encouraging by telling a learner that he or she was not like their peers.

While reflecting on organizations in which you have worked, describe an organizational policy or practice that affirms this guiding principle.

_____

_____

_____

_____

Describe an instructional behavior of yours or of someone you know that illustrates this principle.

_____

_____

_____

_____

The family, as defined by each culture, is the primary system of support in the education of children. It has been our experience and observation that the traditional relationship between home and school is to place most of the responsibilities for involvement with parents or guardians. Cultural Proficiency provides a lens by which teachers, parents or guardians, and administrators find authentic ways to engage in culturally proficient practices to support student achievement. Traditional approaches to parent involvement have parents or guardians coming to the school to demonstrate their care and concern for their children within the school setting. Culturally proficient practice assumes the school setting includes the community and parents.

Furthermore, we observe that educators and parents or guardians often use the term *parent participation* in very different ways. The term often takes on different meanings when school people and the parents or guardians are from different ethnic, racial, immigrant status, faith, or socioeconomic cultural groups. Lawson (2003) coined the terms *communitycentric* and *schoolcentric* to describe these contrasting perceptions.

- *Communitycentric.* "Parents involved in activities that meet the basic needs of their children as going to school well fed, rested, and clean."
- *Schoolcentric.* "Parents involved in activities that are structured and defined for parents by schools." (p. 79)

Educators who pursue and effect meaningful partnerships between the parents and schools are sensitive, respectful, and caring people willing to learn about the culture of the community, its challenges, and its positive opportunities. These educators work with parents and guardians to understand historical, economic, and political barriers that have impeded progress in school-community relations. It is through understanding barriers and in recognizing the positive aspects of the parents' cultures that respect and trust are built.

Learning about barriers and the positive aspects of students' cultures leads to important learning, such as that there are multiple definitions of family. Family is not a one-definition configuration. Culturally proficient educators are aware of many configurations—single parent, multiple-generation extended family, same-gender parents, foster care, and residential care homes. Whatever the configuration for the children in our schools, their family is their family.

REFLECT

Think about students in your classroom or school who have parents or guardians who you consider engaged with their child's education or engaged as leaders in the school. What words do you use to describe them?

_____

_____

_____

_____

Now think about students whose parents and guardians are not engaged. What words do you use to describe them?

_____

_____

_____

_____

Take a moment and think about how you have reached out to the not-engaged parents/guardians. How could you reach out differently? If you could have five minutes with them, what would you want to know about them and their aspirations for their child?

_____

_____

_____

_____

_____

_____

The diverse thought patterns of cultural groups are equally valid and influence how problems are defined and solved. Family and community are defined by culture and may be the primary point of intervention and mechanism for support. They are defined by culture and may differ within groups as well as between groups. It is important to remember that family and community priorities may differ from those of the school or classroom. Recognizing these differences will make it easier to engage in meaningful conversations with families and community members.

REFLECT

While reflecting on organizations in which you have worked, describe an organizational policy or practice that affirms this guiding principle.

_____

_____

_____

_____

_____

Describe an instructional behavior of yours or of someone you know that illustrates this principle.

_____

_____

_____

_____

_____

_____

The absence of cultural competence anywhere is a threat to competent services everywhere. The essential elements of Cultural Proficiency provide the standards for culturally competent behaviors of individuals and organizations. These standards establish guidelines for engaging with your colleagues, the learners in your classroom, and the communities from which the learners come. If we educators are to create an environment that supports and fosters the achievement of all learners, then we must consider everything that effects that environment. The first guiding principle states that culture is a predominant force. If we seek to ignore or deny the effect of this force on our work, then anything we do will inadequately respond to the needs of our learners and their communities.

REFLECT

Remembering the definition for culture (see Chapter 1), are there aspects of your work, or your organization's culture that you perceive as absent of cultural influences?

_____

_____

_____

_____

_____

While reflecting on organizations in which you have worked, describe an organizational policy or practice that affirms this guiding principle.

_____

_____

_____

_____

Describe an instructional behavior of yours or of someone you know that illustrates this principle.

_____

_____

_____

_____

GO DEEPER

Praxis, as you saw in Chapter 1, is the integration of one's theory about a particular field with one's practice in that field. How would you describe your praxis? What are the values that shape and inform your practice? How do your personal values relate to the values of Cultural Proficiency? What are the apparent values of your school or organization? Are they in conflict or congruence with your values? Are they aligned with the values of Cultural Proficiency?

_____

_____

_____

_____

_____

5 Barriers to Cultural Proficiency

Far from creating independent thinkers, schools have always, throughout history, played an institutional role in a system of control and coercion. And once you are well educated, you have already been socialized in ways that support the power structure, which in turn, rewards you immensely.

—Noam Chomsky[1]

GET CENTERED

Think about the last time you were frustrated in your classroom. What kept you from doing your best work? What barriers may have kept the learners from doing their best work?

_____

_____

_____

_____

ENTITLEMENT AND RESISTANCE TO CHANGE

In a culturally proficient organization, effective instructors have a profound knowledge about the subject matter, as well as the ability to teach it. At a minimum, they have a well-developed philosophy of teaching and can readily use a wide variety of instructional strategies to convey what they know of the content. Perhaps more

---

[1]Sennett (2004), p. 27.

important, they effectively interact with learners. From a culturally proficient perspective, however, effective instructors also must have reflected on the barriers to Cultural Proficiency.

The chief barriers to Cultural Proficiency are a lack of awareness of the need to adapt, a sense of entitlement, and institutionalized systems of oppression. Being *unaware of the need to adapt* means not recognizing the need to make personal and organizational changes in response to the diversity of the people within the learning environment. A person creates such a barrier by believing that the only ones who need to change and adapt are the "others"—the ones who are "not like us." A person who has a *sense of entitlement* believes that all the personal achievements and societal benefits that she or he enjoys were accrued solely on her or his individual merit and quality of character. *Systems of oppression* include institutionalized racism, sexism, ableism, and heterosexism, where no overt rules or policies are in place, but members of certain groups are marginalized or experience subtle, but profound discrimination.

These barriers emanate from the assumption that the successes a person has enjoyed as an instructor or learner are available to everyone else in the same way they were available to that person. The barriers are built on at least five assumptions:

1. All people have access to knowledge, skills, and attitudes in the same manner and quality.

2. All people in the classroom or training room relate to everyone else the way they related to the instructor when he or she was a learner.

3. It doesn't matter whether the students are members of a historically entitled population (e.g., propertied white men) or of a historically oppressed group.

4. It doesn't matter whether the students are successful in this society (e.g., Latina professional) or are less so (e.g., poor white male high school dropout).

5. The instructor has tremendous power and equal potential for influence over all the learners in the environment, regardless of the students' background or experiences or current situation.

Most people have not taken the time to thoroughly examine the basis for their assumptions, values, and beliefs. However, they recognize when they feel under attack. Their initial response usually is to blindly defend what has always been there. That is often the case with attitudes toward people who differ from the dominant group. The repose to these barriers is often anger and guilt.

> LuAnn Steiner, a sixth-grade teacher at Pine Hills Middle School, is chairing the first meeting of the Committee for Culturally Proficient Instruction. Several committee members arrived early and are conversing over coffee and cookies while LuAnn and the staff complete the setup for the meeting.

Stu Montgomery, a longtime math teacher, joins the group and observes several posters and quotations placed in the room as part of the environment for the committee meeting: "Look at this room," he says. "I guess we're going to hear the 'I Have a Dream' speech again today. I get tired of hearing how bad things are for some groups. It's not my fault that some white families held slaves before the Civil War."

"Nobody said it was your fault, Stu," replies Andy, a fellow math teacher. "No need to feel guilty about something we had no control over."

Arlene, a social studies teacher, cannot let this moment pass. "Well, you two are always defending yourselves. Our black kids need to learn what the real history is so they can make up their own minds about the world, not just learn the one way that you want them to see it."

LuAnn decides that this was a good time to start the meeting. "Well, it sounds like we have a lot to talk about today. Cultural Proficiency will help us frame our conversations to move beyond the anger and guilt that we feel. Let's get started. While this anger or guilt you are expressing may be normal, if one chooses to stay at that level, it rarely results in deeper learning. However, if it is viewed as an indicator that you are on the verge of deeper learning, it may help us on our journey toward Cultural Proficiency. Are you willing to join us in this conversation?"

REFLECT

Think about a group with which you are not as effective as you would like to be. Perhaps you believe you are not maximally effective with African American women, Latino men, lesbians, European American men, people with AIDS, or lawyers. Write a brief description of this group. Remember that almost everyone holds stereotypical views of members of other groups.

Now write two or three assumptions or beliefs that you hold about members of that group. For instance, if you selected African Americans, you may write that you have doubts about their academic abilities. If you selected gay men and lesbians, you may write about your perception that they have promiscuous lifestyles. If you selected lawyers, you may describe them as money grubbers. Take a few minutes and write your assumptions and beliefs, and what you know to be your biases.

_____

_____

_____

_____

Remember that your assumptions and beliefs serve as filters when working with groups that differ culturally from your own group. Knowing and acknowledging such assumptions and beliefs is an important initial step in the journey toward becoming culturally proficient. Look at your list again, adding to it as more thoughts come to you. Write first, then talk with a trusted colleague. How do you think your beliefs, assumptions, and biases influence the way you teach and the environment you create in your classroom?

_____

_____

_____

_____

Figure 5.1 The Process of Change

Phase of the Change Process	Characteristic Emotions	Individual Challenges	Organization Challenges
Release the old **Endings**	■ Denial, shock ■ Anger, hostility ■ Elation, relief, excitement ■ Disbelief ■ Confusion ■ Disappointment ■ Grief, sense of loss	■ Accept the reality of change ■ Release attachment to people and to the old ways of doing things ■ Acknowledge losses	■ Create the need for change
Change **Transition** *Change*	■ Resistance ■ Sabotage ■ Depression ■ Support ■ Facilitation ■ Resignation ■ Humor ■ Denial ■ Excitement ■ Frustration	■ Review what has been learned in the past ■ Overcome resistance ■ Commit to the future ■ Connect with the transition	■ Communicate a vision of the future ■ Dismantle old systems ■ Mobilize commitment to the new vision ■ Stabilize transition management
Beginnings *Embrace the new*	■ Fear ■ Exploration ■ Resolution ■ Commitment ■ Excitement ■ Resistance ■ Anger ■ Disillusionment ■ Anxiety	■ Master new routines ■ Learn new cultural norms ■ Embrace the new situation	■ Institutionalize the change ■ Reward and reinforce the new systems

Adapted from William Bridges:
Transitions: Making Sense of Life's Changes
Managing Transitions: Making the Most of Change

Organizational change and personal transformations are processes that usually take longer than one expects. Moreover, change doesn't start with trying something new, it begins by recognizing that one must stop or modify one's current way of doing things. Sometimes that means losing or letting go of something that, if not important, is familiar and comfortable. We often hear from our clients: What is broken? Why do we have to change? Our most frequent response is that you are not broken, you are growing.

If you are going to get new furniture, you have to give up the comfortable old, lumpy couch. If you are going to wear new slippers, those tattered old ones need to go. If you are going to earnestly work to become a culturally proficient instructor, you may need to let go of some commonly held beliefs, tried-and-true practices, or generally accepted attitudes toward your students and their families.

William Bridges (2004, 2009), a consultant who specializes in transitions, suggests that the process of change is endings, transitions, and beginnings. Graphically, we see change as represented in Figure 5.1.

REFLECT

What must I release in order to change? What do I miss? What will I miss as I seek to become culturally proficient?

_____

_____

_____

_____

_____

_____

THE DOMINANT CULTURE

Some people are uncomfortable with the term *dominant group*, particularly when they do not feel dominant or powerful. If you never have to think about the groups you are in, if cultural identify is not made an issue for you by others, you are probably a member of the dominant group. That means you have privileges that you didn't earn and probably didn't ask for just because you are a member of that group.

- In a diverse environment there are *dominant groups* and *oppressed or marginalized groups.* The dominant group sets the norms for interactions and often names the oppressed, marginalized groups.
- People who are in a dominant group are often unaware of the advantages they may have because the cultural rules benefit them.
- Another term for dominant group is *mainstream culture.*

Every group comes with certain privileges or entitlements. However dominant cultures have the power to name and oppress others. You may be the dominant in your family or social group. Your occupation, social group, or organization may be a dominant organization. Although you may not be a dominant person, you may belong to a dominant group.

- Almost everyone belongs to a dominant group. It could be in your family, a social group, or in your organization.
- Some people belong to many dominant groups.
- In the United States, the dominant cultures include people of northern and western European descent, people whose sexuality is perceived as straight, and men.

REFLECT

Do you belong to any dominant cultures? What might be some of the dominant groups to which you belong?

Who are the dominant groups at your school, in the classroom, among your colleagues?

_____

_____

_____

_____

TARGETS AND AGENTS

One way of looking at dominant cultures and understanding microaggressions is by understanding targets and agents. Simply put, *agents* are the perpetrators and *targets* are the intended or unintended objects of the agents' negative attention. But it is more complicated than that because a person can be a target in one setting and an agent in another. Those of us who are dominant in our groups can become agents; those of us who are in dominant cultural groups are in *agent groups.*

A target is the person who always gets picked on and laughed at. A *target group* is one that is the object of ridicule and demeaning stereotypes. People in target groups often perceive members of agent groups as prejudiced or biased. People in agent groups often assume people in target groups are all exactly like the negative stereotypes held about the target people.

- Agents pick on, objectify, and oppress others—people who are in their cultures and people who are members of other cultural groups.
- You can be a member of a dominant group and not behave as an agent, but you may be perceived as an agent.
- People or groups that are the objects of agent attacks are called *targets.*
- A target can be in a target group or a low status member of a dominant group.

In schools, agents are often called bullies. Students bully one another, teachers target, or bully, their students. Sometimes teachers are bullied by their colleagues.

REFLECT

Do you *feel* like a target in any of the groups to which you belong?
Are you *perceived* as an agent in any of your groups?
How do students get targeted at your school?

_____

_____

_____

_____

MICROAGGRESSIONS

Becoming Culturally Proficient is often contextualized. What is appropriate in one environment may be highly inappropriate in another. Behavior that is appropriate at a party may be highly offensive in the work setting. To be culturally proficient you have to assess the environment and determine the cultural expectations for that particular setting. To be a diverse and inclusive organization means that you share the cultural expectations with newcomers, instead of waiting for them to figure them out, or teach students the cultural expectations of the classroom, instead of punishing them because they don't know the rules.

In any setting, you may witness practices or behaviors that by themselves may be slightly questionable or not even noticed, but are experienced as microaggressions. They are wrong, but often, when the target complains, their protests are dismissed as inconsequential or they are judged as overly sensitive. Comments that imply that a minority person only got the job because of affirmative action, that a woman is overemotional, or that someone who has cerebral palsy looks stupid are microaggressions. Derald Wing Sue (2010) has documented the many microaggressions experienced by students in classrooms and counseling settings.

- *Macro*aggressions are obviously wrong and offensive behaviors or policies.
- *Micro*aggressions are often treated as isolated incidents. Violators may not even know they did something wrong.
- Because they are often missed, and usually repeated over time, microaggressions become very egregious.
- Microaggressions occur even as one works to become culturally proficient. They may be unintentional slights or awkward attempts to acknowledge one's value for diversity.

Figure 5.2   Understanding Microagressions

Reactive Behaviors and Policies The goal is tolerance.			Proactive Behaviors and Policies The goal is transformation.		
Cultural Destruction	Cultural Incapacity	Cultural Blindness	Cultural Precompetence	Cultural Competence	Cultural Proficiency
Macroaggressions			Microaggressions		

REFLECT

Can you think of examples of language or behaviors that may be perceived by the targets in your group as microaggressions? Where would these incidents fall along the Cultural Proficiency continuum? (Use Figure 5.2 as a point of reference.)

_____

_____

_____

_____

A SHORT SOCIOLOGY LESSON

Many people describe U.S. society as a dominant group of "just plain Americans" and a diverse group of "minorities." *Minorities* are generally those ethnic and social groups that have a history of oppression in the United States. At the same time, it is important to differentiate two kinds of minorities: *castelike groups,* those whose social status rarely changes (e.g., African Americans and Native Americans), and *oppressed immigrant groups* (e.g., Irish and Italian laborers), who assimilated into dominant society after two or three generations (Ogbu, 1978).

It is significant to note that Ogbu's description of *castelike minorities* caused a stir, particularly in academic circles, that persists. Mithun (1979) held that other cultural groups, such as women and Chinese or Jewish persons, have high motivation in the face of restrictions on their professional mobility. Ito (1979) was sympathetic to Ogbu's thesis and faulted schools for the use of compensatory and preventive programs that do not address underlying issues of ineffective curricula and instructional practices. Rist (1979) referred to Ogbu, along with de Tocqueville and Myrdal, and their *perceptive critiques of American race relations* (p. 93). Rist opined that Ogbu's caste thesis is provocative and generally persuasive, but he cautiously noted that school integration had not had time, as of his writing in 1979, to demonstrate an effect on black student achievement. Today we have the advantage of historical perspective and know the achievement gap persists, despite a variety of formats for school integration.

Castelike minorities were brought to the United States against their will or were subjugated during the European migration to North America. As such, these groups endured centuries of legalized racism—slavery, Jim Crow laws, confinement to reservations, and internment camps. Although many people from these groups have been successful in our society, as a group they are overrepresented in the lowest socioeconomic classes, and they are the targets of race-based hatred and discrimination. Oppressed immigrant groups were confined to menial, hard-labor tasks during the nineteenth and twentieth centuries, and like the castelike minorities, they had to resort to legal means to ensure their basic rights. In contrast to the castelike minorities, however, their second and third generations have begun to experience greater success in this country's economic and political arenas.

European immigrant groups also experienced discrimination and deprivation during their first years in the United States. However, European immigrant groups found that as they entered into their second and third generations, they became "white" or "American." These were the Americans who were embraced by the great American melting pot. Although members of castelike groups and oppressed immigrant groups can rightfully point to the hard work their ancestors performed to succeed in the United States (often referred to as "pulling oneself up by one's bootstraps"), European Americans represent the largest proportion of successes—those who moved into the middle and upper social classes in U.S. society. This is the result of hard work, good fortune in some cases, and sometimes the systematic oppression visited on castelike and immigrant groups. Edward Ball (1998) described this process well:

> No one among the Balls talked about how slavery helped us, but whether we acknowledged it or not, the powers of our ancestors were still in hand.

Although our social franchise had shrunk, it had nevertheless survived. If we did not inherit money, or land, we received a great fund of cultural capital, including prestige, a chance at education, self-esteem, a sense of place, mobility, even (in some cases) a flair for giving orders. And it was not only "us," the families of former slave owners, who carried the baggage of the plantations. By skewing things so violently in the past, we had made sure that our cultural riches would benefit all white Americans.

. . . At the same time, the slave business was a crime that had not fully been acknowledged. It would be a mistake to say that I felt guilt for the past. A person cannot be culpable for the acts of others, long dead, that he or she could not have influenced. Rather than responsible, I felt accountable for what had happened, called on to try to explain it. I also felt shame about the broken society that had washed up when the tide of slavery receded. (pp. 13–14)

Ball raises several important concepts. First, he and members of his family benefited from a system that preceded them by generations. It just makes sense that when benefits are denied to one group of people, they accrue to others. Think about it. Those benefits that are denied to one group do not disappear. If one group is systematically denied access to education while other groups have access to education, the latter groups are much more likely to succeed socially and economically.

Second, Ball introduces the concept of guilt. In our workshops, we often observe that when confronted with these ideas for the first time, many people experience guilt or anger. If you are feeling resentful or defensive now, you may be realizing that some of your education has been incomplete. Resentfulness expressed as anger and defensiveness resulting from guilt is a legitimate feeling. Anger and guilt can immobilize you as an instructor and can impede you from seeing your entitlement. Instead, as LuAnn Steiner stated earlier in this chapter, experiencing these very human feelings can indicate you are on the verge of deeper learning. The unrest or discomfort you may feel is a signal that you are shifting away from seeking external, stereotypic reasons for why learners are not successful to pursuing an internal focus on what you need to learn to do differently as an instructor.

REFLECT

Now that you have this information, what can you do with it? We do not wish to fan the flames of anger or guilt, but we do want you to consider how this realization informs and forms your practice as an instructor.

_____

_____

_____

_____

The focus of this book is on you, the instructor. Whether you are a member of the dominant group or you are from a minority group, you possess great power as an instructor. As such, you participate in the dominant group and need to be aware of how you potentially hinder or facilitate the learning of others. This ability emanates from your power as an instructor. Whether you are a member of an entitled or a historically oppressed group, you have the capacity and the responsibility to reach out to all learners.

> Carol Song, a newly appointed human relations specialist, is conducting a workshop on conflict resolution for department heads at Tri-Counties Community College. She asks the group, "What is your role in resolving conflicts that originate from cultural misunderstandings in the workplace?"
>
> Alan, a physics instructor, says, "I never really see any conflicts like that among my students. They just come to class to learn."
>
> Carter, an English instructor says, "Sometimes my students write about how they don't like other students because of their lifestyles or values. I just don't make it a topic of discussion during class."
>
> Olivia, who teaches Asian History, adds, "Carol, by asking the question the way that you did, you must have some insight into the role that we as faculty have in resolving conflict. Do you really think we can make much difference with students when they don't get along with students or groups who are different?"
>
> Carol is glad for the chance to explain. "The principle of unintended consequences is at play here. Even though one does not intend to harm another, or to benefit from the harm done to another, when viewed from a systemic process, most of us benefit from the discrimination visited on others in unintentional and unacknowledged ways. The object lesson here is to see, to know, and to experience how one benefits. At the same time, it is important to realize that these benefits accrue in the complete absence of intention and are, usually, so much a part of our life that we are not aware of it."

REFLECT

What are you thinking and feeling now? What questions come to mind for you and your colleagues?

_____

_____

_____

_____

_____

Figure 5.3 Words Often Used to Describe Nondominant Groups and Implied Terms for Dominant Groups

Inferior	Superior
Culturally Deprived	Privileged
Culturally Disadvantaged	Advantaged
Deficient	Normal
Different	Similar
Diverse	Uniform
Third World	First World
Minority	Majority
Underclass	Upper Class
Poor	Middle Class
Unskilled Workers	Leaders

A BARRIER FOR INSTRUCTORS

Stereotypes about castelike and immigrant groups abound in classrooms and training rooms. Our language is a key to understanding how we have been shaped to have certain views. The training room and the school classroom exist in an institutional framework that has not served all students well. Those of us who live and work in these settings have been influenced by societally held assumptions, values, and beliefs about other cultural groups. To fully understand how entitlement creates barriers for some and opportunities for others, you need to see how your language objectifies and dehumanizes people. Language reflects the power relationships in our society. Historically, our society has used language to explain the disparities between oppressed and entitled groups (Lindsey, Nuri Robins, & Terrell, 2009). Figure 5.3 presents some common terms reflecting these disparities.

Each of the terms in the first column describes groups that occupy the oppressed end of the entitlement continuum. These terms are used to explain why students from these groups fail to perform at specified levels. Using these terms gives instructors permission to view a learner, and that person's group, as being unable to achieve. Similarly, these terms free the instructor from considering the institutionalized oppression to which these learners are subjected. It makes it so simple. *They* (whoever *they* are) are not learning because they are incapable of doing so. The unquestioned use of these terms suggests that people of color, who are disproportionately represented on the oppressed end of the continuum, and other oppressed groups suffer from pathological conditions. Unfortunately, this polarity of language and perceptions emanates daily from schools and training rooms. The effect of using terms of oppression is that the focus is on what is wrong with *them*, implying that these "others" must be studied and then fixed.

The terms in the second column, when applied in classrooms and training rooms, describe learners who are part of the dominant culture of our country. The instructor who aspires to be culturally proficient looks at the words in the second column and examines the implications of those terms being used or inferred when interacting with learners who represent the dominant group in our society. That these words are rarely spoken underscores the fact that entitled people do not objectify or name themselves. They only name *others*, people they perceive to differ from themselves.

The use of the terms *disadvantaged* and *deprived*, in their many permutations, implies that there is a norm to which people are compared (Lindsey et al., 2009). There are at least two considerations here. One is that norms are fixed and immutable and that any person or group that fails to measure up to that norm must be deficient in some way. The other is the belief on the part of middle-class America that all groups want to be like them, when many may not. Many groups don't want to do what they perceive as "acting white" (Singham, 1998). The limitation in each of these explanations is that the focus of change is on the learner and not on the instructor. When the focus is on instruction rather than on the perceived, stereotypic capabilities of the learner, achievement results (Chenoweth, 2007; Noguera, 1999; Singham, 1998).

Once instructors take the responsibility to examine their own behaviors, as Carol Song invites us to do in the previous story, then significant progress can be made in identifying institutional barriers and making instructional decisions to benefit learners.

INSTITUTIONAL BARRIERS

Culturally proficient instructors have good command of their subject matter and use a variety of teaching techniques. They see each learner as an individual and express to the learner, in myriad ways, their interest in the learner's success and ability to learn. Instructors know the learner's learning style and teach to that style. They also work with the learner to experiment with, and to become comfortable with, alternative learning styles. In doing so, they recognize that the learner needs to know the information and, by facilitating the learner in alternative learning styles, are preparing the learner to succeed in a variety of settings. Culturally proficient corporate trainers or university professors may not have this intimate knowledge of each learner. Nonetheless, they recognize that learning styles differ and they prepare materials and activities that acknowledge the diverse needs and learning styles of adult learners.

> Al Hernandez recognizes that the way life works for him may not be the way it works for others. He realizes that on his way to the high school one morning, when he stopped at the local coffee shop for his customary scone and double latte, not everyone was welcomed in the same manner. He knows that as a student, he was above average. His teachers expected him to succeed, and if he had not, they would have contacted his parents. He knows that he had more than one teacher who saw has potential and that the encouragement of these teachers contributed mightily to his success. He wants to see the learners in Maple View influenced in the same way.
>
> Helen Williams, a preschool teacher, recognizes that, as an African American, she related well to the African American students when they used to live in the community. Now, she

recognizes that the demographic shift has presented her with students whose first language is other than English. Though she and her students are both members of "minority" groups, she has lots to learn to be an effective instructor for her new students.

Carol Song has always been a good trainer, but she has had to increase the use of high-tech learning games and interactive strategies to tap the experience and interests of new employees.

The culturally proficient instructor believes that when new learners experience difficulties, it is not the learners' cultural behaviors and patterns that are suspect, but rather, it is the instructor's behavior that must change and adapt to meet their needs for learning.

Alicia Alvarez, the director of Training and Staff Development at the Maple View District Office, meets with her supervisor, Alan Roderick, to discuss an upcoming training session. In the past, Alan has provided Alicia with the topics for the training. This time, he plans to do so again: "Alicia, I think the next training session should be, Communication Skills for Teachers, like we did last year."

This year, however, Alicia wants to offer a different approach. "I've been thinking about that topic also, Alan. I looked at the feedback forms from the last session that I did, and the participants asked whether we could do something about the topics of conflict resolution and problem solving at their schools. I think this is important to consider new and different ways to meet the needs of our teachers."

Alan is thoughtful. "But they each have different content areas and different kinds of problems. The communication module is already written and it would be too hard to change it."

Alicia replies, "I've been gathering a variety of materials in each of the content areas. I found a great video that we could use, and we could ask them to create several scenarios about their real problem areas; then we could design activities around those scenarios. I could put a new module together by early next week for you to look at."

"OK, Alicia, I think you are on to something here. Let's try it."

Instructors must commit to ensuring constructive outcomes for all learners. Culturally proficient instructors must be able to see the process of teaching and learning from the social context of the learners. An important component of this teaching-learning dynamic is to see the barriers that exist for some, but not all, learners. When instructors acknowledge and consider these barriers in preparing instructional materials, they provide for more equitable learning opportunities.

Six institutional processes can pose barriers to learning unless a culturally proficient instructor, and organization, overcomes these barriers:

1. *Content:* A curriculum that projects only one cultural experience.

2. *Delivery:* Instruction that emphasizes lower-order thinking skills (memorization, learning by rote, recitation of the one right answer).

3. *Expectations:* Preconceptions based on stereotypical views of the learners.

4. *Assessment:* Evaluation of progress or achievement that is compliance oriented.

5. *Resources:* Culturally inadequate resources that continue and maintain inappropriate policies and practices.

6. *Outside Involvement:* Biased parent and community involvement that caters to the most influential parents and community members; management is not included in the design, delivery, or reinforcement of training programs.

ENGAGE

As you and your colleagues reflect on your places of instruction, ask yourselves: Who benefits most from these six institutional processes that are potential barriers to culturally proficient instruction? What have you observed or heard that supports your answers?

_____

_____

_____

_____

Now, think about yourself as a learner. How does a learning environment that has the barriers described suit you as a learner? How does it pose difficulties for you as a learner?

_____

_____

_____

_____

People who have benefited from such systems are often confused by—or openly hostile to—those who claim that although they have worked hard they have not benefited from the same system. Those who have benefited most from the system of entitlement do not see the need to change the system at all. They see their experiences as the "opportunities" held by everyone. For example, "if I could do it, everyone could do it" and "I worked hard for what I have" are common statements of entitlement. The speaker assumes everyone had the same or similar experiences, or at least the same or similar opportunities. That assumption is dangerous and myopic, and it poses a barrier to Cultural Proficiency. It reflects a lack of awareness of the need to adapt. In contrast, the culturally proficient instructor feels committed to learning what is necessary to teach others. This instructor is able to take those six institutional practices listed above and modify them in ways that make them work as assets for instruction rather than barriers to quality instruction.

Knowing the barriers to effective instruction greatly empowers you as an instructor. These barriers are grounded in historical events and perpetuated in current institutional policies and practices. Nonetheless, as a culturally proficient instructor, it is your responsibility to make the changes in the domain over which you have the most control and influence: your classroom. When you collaborate with others in how you approach your classrooms, you begin the process of shaping the policies and practices of your organizations.

ENGAGE

Review the following six institutional practices. Study the examples, and in the spaces provided, write examples of barriers in your instructional environment for those who differ from the dominant group.

Content Barriers

- A single-perspective curriculum, often represented by a single-text approach.
- A curricular program that segregates diversity as a separate course.
- Tracking of students into segregated classrooms, where they are given content designed in accord with stereotypes about them.
- Use of commercial training materials that aren't customized for a particular group of students and learners.

_____

_____

_____

_____

Delivery Barriers

- Emphasis on basic skills only.
- A passive, teacher-directed learning as only delivery system (i.e., lectures).
- Failure to learn students' names.
- Failure to learn how to pronounce students' names, or changing student's names for convenience.
- Failure to view the cultural background of children as assets.

_____

_____

_____

_____

Expectation Barriers

- Use of models emphasizing innate ability (e.g., bell curve and norm fallacies) instead of efficacy.
- Instruction based on ability grouping only.
- Disproportional referrals of underrepresented groups to special education.
- Expecting training programs to fix whatever problems the instructors have identified.
- Using training to punish instructors for inappropriate behavior.
- Using training as an alternative to adequate supervision and coaching on the job.

_____

_____

_____

_____

Assessment Barriers

- Reliance on a text and basic-skills approach.
- Providing little feedback to learners during the course.
- Data used for compliance purposes, not to inform practice.
- Assessment based on assumptions about "appropriate" learner responses.
- Schoolwide progress assumed when only "bubble" students have made progress.
- Statewide assessments viewed as the single most important assessment tool.
- Summative assessments made without use of formative assessments.

_____

_____

_____

_____

Resource Barriers

- Controlled access to gifted and talented education (GATE) and to advanced placement (AP) instruction.
- In colleges and universities, majors associated with a particular culture or gender.
- Limited access to extracurricular activities.
- Use of paper-and-pen materials rather than the wider range of materials that speaks to diverse learning styles.
- Limited access to technology (e.g., technology reserved for advanced classes).

- Training budgets so small that training departments exist in name only.
- Constraints on workers, either failing to release them for training or making training an onerous addition to their workload because no one else can do their jobs.

_____

_____

_____

_____

Barriers to Organizational or Community Involvement

- The belief that parents who don't come to school do not care about their children.
- Activist parents considered antischool or even antieducation.
- Lack of services from or involvement with the local community.
- Supervisors who send workers to training to "fix" them.
- Executive management totally unaware of the training programs being offered.

_____

_____

_____

_____

GO DEEPER

Over the next few weeks, observe the institutional barriers in the organizations you encounter (e.g., a store, hospital, bank, school, university) that may impede the involvement of all interested parties. Note the examples you find.

_____

_____

_____

_____

_____

6 The Cultural Proficiency Continuum

Learning is more than the acquisition of the ability to think; it is the acquisition of many specialized abilities for thinking about a variety of things.

—L. S. Vygotsky[1]

Think of a time when you observed the inappropriate behavior of your colleagues and chose not to comment. Was your choice related to not knowing what to say? Did you wonder how you could say something without sounding judgmental or self-righteous?

_____

_____

_____

_____

_____

---

[1]Sennett (2004), p. 8.

TOM'S STORY

"Hi, Tom, remember me? I'm Al Hernandez. I called you earlier in the week. Have you got a minute to chat with me?" Al asks Tomas "Tom" Morales, a teacher who serves on the district technology committee.

"Sure, come on in. My class just left, and I was going to grade a few papers, but that can wait. How have you been doing?"

Tom is in his early forties. He is a widowed father of three school-age children. After his wife Lupe's death, Tom tried to remain at Pine Hills Elementary where he and Lupe had taught, but the memories were too painful for him. He requested a transfer to Maple View Elementary School, where they needed an English language learner (ELL) teacher. Tom's parents had emigrated from Cuba, so he spoke Spanish fluently, but he had never taught an ELL class before. Pine Hills Elementary did not have ELL students, so there was not a need for the program there. Tom decided to take the transfer so that he would learn something new himself. His first year at Maple View, on the East Side, was harder than he had thought it would be. His students struggled with reading because they could not speak English. Tom decided it would be better to teach the students to read in Spanish than it would be to try to teach them English and try to teach them to read at the same time. He didn't feel he was very successful, but no one complained. He took a Spanish refresher course over the summer to help him improve his own use of the language.

He decided to take his three children for a two-week trip to Mexico to visit Lupe's relatives. He had never previously visited Mexico, even though Lupe's parents had told them of her relatives there. He hoped the visit would help with the grieving process, allow his children to get to know the rest of their family, and give him opportunities to practice his Spanish.

"How do you like being here at Maple View Elementary School, Tom?" Al feels a little embarrassed about sounding so personal with his first question. "What I mean is, I know you taught over at Pine Hills for a few years and just wanted to get your perspective on the 'East Side/West Side' talk from the newspaper. You've seen it from both sides of town, so to speak."

"You've asked a really tough question, you know." Tom seems hesitant at first. "I'm not sure I can shed much light on the subject. The kids on the West Side just seem to have it easier than the kids over here. I mean those kids come to school with everything they need. Kids over here seem to be missing out—not missing school, just missing opportunities. They don't want charity. We don't need handouts for our kids. We need access to the best curriculum and materials and technology. We need opportunity. The kids have the potential. We hold the promise."

"Would you be willing to work with me on a community project that will help us to keep that promise, together?" Al asks Tom, not even sure of what he is proposing.

"Count me in," Tom says. He then asks a tough question of his own: "But where do we start?"

Al and Tom decide to continue the work that Al has started. They make a list of names of people in the community who would have information and experiences to help them piece together the East Side puzzle. Once they have made their list, Al and Tom each take several names and start the interviews. After two weeks, they review their findings with each other. Al began his interviews with one of his colleagues at the high school, Charlene Brennaman. They began by asking questions about how they describe and talk about the students and the community they serve.

The Cultural Proficiency continuum provides a context, or frame of reference, by which you can describe organizations and individuals. You can use the Cultural Proficiency continuum as a tool for depicting aspects of your organizational culture's approach, as well as your personal approach, to issues of diversity. In an organizational context, you can use the continuum to explain how your organization uses existing policies and practices. On a personal level, you can use it to describe specific events or situations.

The continuum provides language for substantive conversations about your organization's policies and practices. For instance, in a given school or classroom, responses to the following questions, would yield rich information about its prevailing culture.

- When achievement is examined by demographic groups (e.g., gender, race, or ethnicity), are learners succeeding similarly across groups? Why or why not?
- Does the examination of instructor-learner response patterns across demographic groups reveal differences in frequency of, duration of, or prompts for higher-level thinking? If so, why?
- Will all learners find themselves represented in the curriculum? Why or why not?

Responses to *why* questions can be plotted along the continuum. The subsequent conversations allow better understanding of learning environments and the organization or classroom culture. Similarly, continuing self-examination will provide you with the opportunity to examine your own policies, practices, and behaviors that include some learners and exclude others. In this way, you may describe how you act out your own inherited and acquired values and behaviors and plot these actions along the continuum.

We urge you to carefully review this continuum before proceeding to the chapters on the essential elements of Cultural Proficiency. We have found in our work with people who are learning to use Cultural Proficiency as a conceptual model that they are better able to effectively apply the essential elements of Cultural Proficiency to their own classrooms and organizations after they have had an opportunity to understand the Cultural Proficiency continuum. By understanding and internalizing the deepest implications of the continuum, you will be better able to appreciate and understand how to use this tool for organizational change. For change to be effective, you must begin where you and your organization are, not where you want yourself or your organization to be.

In using the continuum to describe your own instructional practices or organizational policies, we urge you not to use it to label yourself or your organization at fixed points; human and organizational cultures are too complex to be relegated to fixed points. Each organization and instructor can usually be represented as a range of points on the continuum, points that vary with the situations in which they find themselves. While avoiding overall labels, use the continuum to study singular events in your classroom or in your organization, to examine specific policies or particular behaviors, or to begin conversations that analyze your organizational culture or your personal development. In doing so, use the range of points as starting places and benchmarks by which to assess progress and direction. Bear in mind that movement along the continuum may not be a fluid progression, continually gliding along in one direction toward Cultural Proficiency. As with all other aspects of learning, you'll experience fits and starts, great leaps forward, occasional slides backward, and jerky halfhearted movements ahead again.

POINTS ALONG THE CULTURAL PROFICIENCY CONTINUUM

There are six points on the continuum, moving from cultural destructiveness to Cultural Proficiency (see Figure 6.1).

Cultural Destructiveness

Cultural destructiveness is any policy, practice, or behavior that effectively eliminates all vestiges of another peoples' cultures. It may be manifested through an organization's policies and practices or through an individual's values and behaviors. Sometimes, these destructive actions occur intentionally, but more often, they are unwittingly carried out as part of prevailing practice. Systems of legalized oppression are clear examples. Legalized oppression includes the system of slavery that accompanied the African Diaspora, Jim Crow laws of segregation, the reservation system established and maintained for Native Americans, the boarding school system that forced Native American children to be separated from their families, the

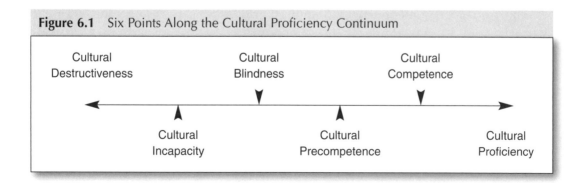

Figure 6.1 Six Points Along the Cultural Proficiency Continuum

internment of Japanese American citizens during World War II, and the many means by which people have been denied the use of their native languages.

In addition to these egregious examples are less obvious, but no less pernicious, instances of cultural destructiveness. For instance, history textbooks used in some of the most prominent school districts do little to explain the origins of modern racism. Thankfully, they do a better job than the textbooks of the 1950s and 1960s in revealing the historical racism underlying the enslavement of Africans and African Americans and the subjugation of Native Americans. Nonetheless, current textbooks still do little to link historical racism to its modern counterpart. The effects of modern racism on people of color is generally well described, but most textbooks do little to link modern racism to historical white complicity in the perpetuation of racism. According to a respected analyst of history textbooks, James Loewen (1995), the explanation of this link from history to today would give students a perspective on "what caused racism in the past, what perpetuates it today, and how it might be reduced in the future" (p. 138).

In these cases of more subtle forms of cultural destructiveness, textbook authors and other educators fail to show the numerous benefits that members of the dominant society have derived from the subjugation of other people. As a result, members of the dominant group do not know the link between history and modern events, so they readily avoid becoming involved in eliminating contemporary systems of oppression. Thus, cultural destructiveness not only perpetuates the negative effects of oppression on nondominant groups but also seems to justify a distorted view of reality on the part of groups that benefit from these same systems of oppression.

Another aspect of cultural destructiveness is the absence of many people and events in most school curricula, which leads to the question: "What happened to our history and literature books?" Whether intentional or unintentional, when textbook authors and curriculum developers omit entirely or neglect or distort the contributions of entire cultural groups, they are engaging in cultural destructiveness.

Some people worry that to raise these issues is to engage in divisiveness and negativity. That reaction only perpetuates cultural destructiveness. Just as we don't help alcoholics by denying their alcohol-related problems and behavior, it doesn't help our nation to heal its divisions by ignoring entire cultures or cultural groups. Though one may try to ignore these problems, they continue to pose a source of concern and embarrassment.

The oppression of people of color and other nondominant groups in the United States damages society. At present, the dominant society often appears to be unaware of the need to adapt and respond to the many incidents of oppression that exist. This denial tears at the moral fiber of U.S. society.

To deny the experiences of all members of society is to deny the barriers to Cultural Proficiency discussed in the previous chapter. Acknowledging these barriers is not to deny or excuse current efforts at accomplishment. Rather, to recognize barriers creates opportunities to learn for members of both the dominant group and the nondominant or "minority" groups. In doing so, members of the dominant group become aware of the unacknowledged benefits they derive from systems of oppression and then choose to accept their personal responsibility for perpetuating those systems as a way of life. Members of "minority" groups become fully aware of these systems and choose not to be perpetual victims; they fully understand the oppression that arises from being viewed, by themselves and by others, as victims and instead they choose self-determination as a way of life.

For more examples of cultural destructiveness, read the works of Andrews and Gates (1999), Carmichael and Hamilton (1967), Franklin and Moss (1988), Lindsey (1999), Loewen (1995), Ogbu (1978), Takaki (1993), and Vigil (1980). Each of these works may extend your understanding of the historical dynamics that have led to the many current, unresolved issues related to diversity. These unresolved issues beg to be addressed by those who aspire to Cultural Proficiency.

REFLECT

Write your reaction to what you have just read about cultural destructiveness. List additional examples of cultural destructiveness.

_____

_____

_____

_____

In an eleventh-grade course in the humanities, combining U.S. history and literature, the teacher, Ms. Linda Catelli, has had the students read *Voyage of the Damned and Judgment at Nuremberg*. Her goal is to have the students develop an understanding of the horrors of war. She plans, next week, to use the video *Saving Private Ryan.*

"Well, in these last two weeks we have covered a lot of information! Some of it, I am sure, you found troubling," Ms. Catelli says to the class.

"You know, Ms. Catelli," Trent says, "I think you believe all this BS, but I am here to tell you that the holocaust did not happen, the international Jewish conspiracy has blown World War II way out of proportion."

"What the hell is the international Jewish conspiracy?" Rachel squeals. "You must be crazy."

"Hey, who are you calling crazy?" Trent retorts. "Haven't you heard of the New World Order?"

"Trent! Rachel! Knock it off." Ms. Catelli tries to regain order. "I am tired of you two arguing during every single class. Trent, where did you get those outrageous ideas?"

"On the Internet! I am tired of the biased information that we get in this school. It is always about how so-called minorities have been exploited. I have a couple of websites that tell the real history. Did you know that Hitler was only trying to preserve a way of life, and communists and Jews were undermining that way of life? Did you know that Martin Luther King was a communist dedicated to the overthrow of our country? Did you know that the welfare system is the way that minorities are undermining the economy of this country? Did you know that I can study hard and graduate from this damned school, but I won't be able to get a job because I am a white male?"

REFLECT

What are the issues of cultural destructiveness in the preceding story?

_____

_____

_____

_____

What assumptions have Ms. Catelli made? What assumptions have Trent made?

_____

_____

_____

_____

If you were Ms. Catelli, how would you handle this situation? What would you do the next time your class met?

_____

_____

_____

_____

REFLECT

Reflecting on organizations in which you have been employed, describe an organizational policy or practice that illustrates cultural destructiveness. Describe a behavior or value of yours or of someone you know that illustrates cultural destructiveness.

_____

_____

_____

_____

_____

Cultural Incapacity

Cultural incapacity is any policy, practice, or behavior that presumes one culture is superior to others. In culturally incapacitating organizations, employees behave in ways that disempower people who differ from them culturally. Cultural incapacity tolerates differences without valuing diversity. Consequently, members of the dominant culture relate to others based on negative stereotypes and make policies based on a token acceptance of differences. In culturally incapacitating classrooms, the most frequent illustrations of disempowerment arise from holding low expectations for learners. These low expectations may be held by instructors, based on their perceptions of various cultural groups. Lowered expectations also result in tokenism.

Thus, disempowerment is an interactive phenomenon in which a dominant group renders another group powerless and the nondominant group perceives (and reinforces) its own powerlessness by internalizing its own oppression. Most people are familiar with the actions of the dominant group; although they may view those actions with disdain, they are relatively easier to understand than the actions of the nondominant group. Paulo Freire (1987, 1999) discusses this behavior of nondominant groups in his concept of internalized oppression. *Internalized oppression* occurs when members of an oppressed group take on the attitudes or worldview of their oppressor. They see themselves as inferior and often treat one another in the same demeaning way as their external oppressor has treated them.

REFLECT

Carefully consider the following examples of *cultural incapacity*—lowered expectations or internalized oppression.

- Have you ever been aware of a female learner saying that she is not good in math because girls don't do well in math? Have you heard male learners make such a comment? Have you or your colleagues ever made such a statement? How did you react?

_____

_____

_____

_____

- Have you ever been reluctant to work with learners from a particular cultural group because of your perception that they are not good students? Have you heard this from colleagues? Have you heard it from other learners? Describe your reactions.

_____

_____

_____

_____

- Have you been aware of colleagues or other learners who ascribe stereotypic labels to learners because their primary language is other than English? Do you think they would respond in the same way if someone's accent was French or Danish? What if it was Arabic or Swahili? Why or why not?

_____

_____

_____

_____

- Have you heard colleagues or other learners excuse the low academic performance of learners in a nondominant group by pointing to the one person who is an outstanding example in that group? How did you react in this situation?

_____

_____

_____

_____

REFLECT

Create your own list of examples of lowered expectations, tokenism, or use of stereotypes to characterize a group or a group member's behavior.

_____

_____

_____

_____

Now, write your reactions to the information about cultural incapacity.

_____

_____

_____

_____

Add the following to the list of examples that you have developed.

Alicia Alvarez, the director of Training and Staff Development at the University Medical Center (UMC), is initiating a new program for aspiring managers. At this facility, the intern physicians tend to be males and females from the State University Medical Institute and from Asia and South America. Conversely, most of the managers are white males who have come from a prominent, private university known for its MBA program. The medical center has taken pride in its entry-level managers being sought after by hospitals throughout the country, which has added to the prestige of UMC. The board of directors, at its last meeting, decided that it had to be more proactive in recruiting members of underrepresented groups into management positions. They made it perfectly clear that this was not to be a closeted affirmative action program and that they wanted all candidates to be fully qualified, both academically and experientially. Alicia has taken this new directive to heart in recruiting candidates into the Career Ladder Program (CLP). CLP is limited to fifteen candidates annually, and the current class is the most diverse class ever, comprising both women and men: seven European American, four Asian Pacific, two African American, and two Central American candidates.

At the orientation session, Alicia says, "This is such an exciting year. This is the most diverse class in the history of CLP. As you know, this movement toward diversity is a directive from the board."

"Excuse me, what do you mean by 'directive'?" Tanya asks.

"Isn't it obvious?" Paul says. "I mean no disrespect, but don't you find it strange that for several years, people of color, or whatever you're called now, couldn't qualify and now suddenly we are overwhelmed by you people?"

"Hey, why are you so hostile?" Katya jumps in. "We are going to be together for the next twenty weeks, and you already have an attitude."

"Please, everyone!" Alicia says. "Maybe the word *directive* was a misstatement on my part."

"You can call it a misstatement if you want," Paul says, "but I think it is probably a slip of the truth."

REFLECT

What are the issues of cultural incapacity in the story? What assumptions has Alicia made? What about Paul? What do you make of Katya's comment?

_____

_____

_____

_____

_____

If you were Alicia, how would you handle this situation? What would you do at the next meeting?

_____

_____

_____

_____

_____

REFLECT

Think about organizations in which you have been employed and describe an organizational policy or practice that reflects cultural incapacity. Describe a behavior or value of yours or of someone you know that illustrates cultural incapacity.

_____

_____

_____

_____

Cultural Blindness

Cultural blindness is any policy, practice, or behavior that ignores existing cultural differences or that considers such differences inconsequential. Often, people of goodwill speak proudly of "not seeing color, just seeing human beings." We find this stance the most vexing point on the continuum. People who hold cultural blindness as a goal often fail to observe the effect they are having on others. By not seeing differences and treating everyone alike, one presumes that the dominant cultural norms are equally beneficial for all.

Most culturally blind instructors do not intend to harm others or to benefit from the harm done to others. Nonetheless, from a systemic standpoint, most people from the dominant cultural group unwittingly and unintentionally benefit from the various forms of oppression that affect people from nondominant cultural groups. Moreover, when members of a dominant group value cultural blindness, they cause further unintended harm by contributing to the sense of invisibility experienced by members of nondominant groups. Often, people who value cultural blindness don't realize how their blindness leads to a sense of invisibility for those belonging to nondominant cultural groups.

Another example of cultural blindness is the American melting pot metaphor. Such a mythical aim may have been desirable in the late nineteenth and early twentieth centuries for some immigrants from eastern and southern Europe. However, many Americans were never "meltable." The melting pot was neither desirable nor attainable for millions of Americans, now or in the past. These Americans have been the victims of legalized oppression, systematically denied access to the opportunities available to most other Americans because of their ethnicity.

Cultural invisibility and blindness comes in many forms.

- The trainer of a conflict management class says, "I don't see color, I just see participants in my workshop."
- In my classroom I don't see color or race. I treat all students the same.
- As superintendent, I take one day per week and visit classrooms throughout our school district. I have to tell you, after visiting any given classroom, I can't tell you the ethnic, racial, or gender composition of the classroom.

- An instructor takes a course in African American history in his graduate program with the intention of learning more about the accomplishments, trials, and tribulations of African Americans. None of the information repeats what he learned from his undergraduate major in U.S. history.
- An administrator who takes a food-fun-and-fiestas or heroes-holidays-and-haute-cuisine approach to diversity declares, "Diversity is about celebrating what we have in common. All that other anger stuff just doesn't matter!"
- A fifth-grade teacher says, "I really want to be fair to all my students, so I treat them all alike."
- A college professor asks, "Why all the fuss about ethnic studies? In America, we have one history. Why not just focus on American history?"

In each of these examples, the instructors failed to note the difference between equity and equality. The inability to distinguish between these two fundamental concepts is characteristic of the culturally blind instructor. *Equality* refers to having identical privileges, status, or rights, regardless of the individual's needs, current situation, background, or context. *Equity* refers to being just, impartial, and fair, taking into consideration individual differences (Boyer, 1983). For years, many police departments and fire departments had minimum height and weight requirements that they applied *equally* to all applicants. Because the average man differed from the average woman in terms of height and weight, these requirements were not *equitable* because they disproportionately barred more women than men from entering these departments. Instead, these departments now more *equitably* require that all their prospective employees pass minimum tests of physical strength, endurance, and flexibility that men and women can both work to achieve.

In an educational environment, the Scholastic Assessment Test (SAT) is designed so that all students are given the same test, under the same conditions, and with the same scoring policies. Hence, everyone has an equal chance of doing well on the SAT. Some students, however, can purchase specialized tutorials, coaching, and test preparation, whereas others cannot buy additional aids in preparing for the test. In fact, many students may have outside factors that limit their ability to perform well (e.g., poor nutrition, lack of sleep, low expectations for doing well, increased environmental stress, inadequate school facilities or materials). For these reasons, students may not have an *equitable* chance of doing well on the SAT, despite the test designers' best intentions to provide an *equal* chance for every student to do well.

Instructors know that the learners who enter the classroom or training room come with different backgrounds and experiences. Effective instructors approach the classroom or training room assuming that each learner arrives with variations in knowledge, skills, and prior educational experiences. These instructors know the learners' educational needs and realize that school curricula usually fail to include multiple perspectives or experiences. Therefore, they strive for equity when addressing the learners' needs for learning new knowledge and skills, and they consider equality to be a worthy, if distant, goal for a future time, when equity has been achieved.

ENGAGE

With your colleagues, discuss these examples of cultural blindness, then create a list of your own examples.

_____

_____

_____

_____

Helen Williams, a gifted and experienced preschool teacher at Maple View Elementary School, directs the school's English learners (EL) program. Helen is widely respected in the community and has been particularly effective in communicating with the parents of children who are English learners. In her role as director, she visits the morning class and observes the new teacher, Bonnie Charlton. Bonnie is a first-year teacher who is working on completing the course work for her state teaching certification. She is entering teaching as a second career. She is enthusiastic about being a teacher and wants to do her very best. Bonnie has confided in Helen that she is concerned about teaching children who don't speak English fluently because she doesn't speak their native language.

"Bonnie," Helen says, "describe your classroom arrangement for me."

"I am so excited about my plan," Bonnie says. "I decided to arrange the American kids and the migrant kids in different groups."

"Talk to me about your rationale," Helen says. "Do they stay separated for the whole day?"

"Well, yes. I want to make sure the others do not hold the American kids back. Actually, this helps me do a better job with the migrant kids."

Helen presses, "I have some concerns about your grouping practices. Let's talk about several different instructional strategies that will support your students and your need to see your students be successful. I'm also curious about your seating chart. Your chart doesn't match the names of the girls and boys assigned to your class."

"Well, as you know I have never taken Spanish, and I find their names to be very hard to pronounce, so I decided to ask all the migrant kids to pick an American name, until I can learn their real names. So, that makes it easier for me."

REFLECT

What are the issues of cultural blindness in this story? What assumptions has Bonnie made? If you were Helen Williams, how would you handle this situation? What would you say next?

_____

_____

_____

_____

REFLECT

Describe your classroom experiences with behaviors or attitudes that reflect cultural blindness.

_____

_____

_____

_____

Reflecting on organizations in which you have been employed, describe an organizational policy or practice that illustrates cultural blindness. Describe a behavior or value of yours or of someone you know that illustrates cultural blindness.

_____

_____

_____

_____

Cultural Precompetence

People and organizations that are _culturally precompetent_ recognize that their skills and practices are limited when interacting with other cultural groups. They may have made some changes in their approaches to the issues arising from diversity, but they are aware that they need assistance and more information. The examples in the following stories encountered by a college instructor, a school district superintendent, and a community college administrator are situations of cultural competence. The common denominator in each case is the realization that what they were doing was not working and they see the need for doing something different.

The Chemistry Professor's Story

A chemistry instructor at State University, Maple View campus, learned that many of his students were immigrants from Portugal. Even though he knew that most of them spoke English fluently, he also knew that they took great pride in their cultural heritage. This was a very new culture to him, even though he had taken a semester of Portuguese in addition to his three years of Spanish language in high school. In an attempt to establish rapport with the students, he decided to pronounce the word *Portuguese* with what he thought would be the appropriate accent. Unfortunately, his Portuguese had a poor Spanish accent, and what the students heard was a word that sounded a lot like an ethnic slur for Portuguese people.

The Superintendent's Story

The superintendent of the Maple View School District was known across the region for being in the forefront of innovations that benefited the education of learners in Maple View. She had taken note that in the previous five years, the number of learners who were not fluent in English had increased dramatically. This increase had presented challenges that they had begun to address during the preceding two years. First, these students were overrepresented in the lowest-ability classes, and their parents were beginning to press for reasons as to why these students were in the "low classes." Second, there were isolated fights between English-speaking and non-English-speaking students at the high school.

The superintendent was concerned that the image of the community was being tarnished when the media described the fist fights as race riots. She knew that many of the parents had invested a lot of money in their homes in the Pine Ridge community and that the schools were a key to keeping property values high. Though the number of incidents at Pine Hills High School remained low, she was quite aware of what had happened in high schools in nearby New Metropolis as populations shifted, and she wanted to prevent riots from igniting in her district. In an effort to keep the concerned parents at bay and to continue her reputation for being on the cutting edge of educational innovation, she decided to have an external group from a prominent consulting firm conduct a human relations audit of the community.

The VP's Story

For several years, the Tri-Counties Community College at Maple View had received funding from the federal government to provide technical support for training retired members of the military service for second careers. Because of the extremely high quality of the program, the placement rate exceeded 95 percent. However, the administrators and faculty working in the program were almost all white, whereas the clerical and technical-support personnel were almost all people of color. In the most recent audit, the granting agency said that there appeared to be serious communication problems between the supervisors and the clerical-technical staff. Although the auditors were silent on the issue of ethnicity in the two levels of program staff, they expressed deep concerns about the communication issues. They indicated in their final report that continued funding would be contingent on satisfactorily responding to these issues.

The governing board of the college suggested to the president that this problem warranted immediate attention. She assigned the matter to the vice president for human resources, Dr. Geraldo "Gerry" Diaz. Gerry saw this as an opportunity to approach the issue on a more systemic level. He sent a request for proposals (RFP) to consultants who had successful track records in working with issues arising from diversity. The major criteria in the RFP were to provide services that addressed the immediate problems of communication and problem solving and thereby addressed the underlying issues.

REFLECT

How does each of the situations you just read reflect cultural precompetence?

_____

_____

_____

_____

_____

_____

Maple View's Ongoing Story

The Maple View School District is in its third year of disaggregating student achievement data. Though this was part of a new statewide initiative, most of the school leaders, both administrators and leaders in the teacher's union, are still struggling with how to best use test data information. Dr. Beatrice Connelly, the assistant superintendent for curriculum and staff development, convenes a committee representing lead teachers and key administrators in the school district. Dr. Lee Kim distributes the fourth-grade and eighth-grade test scores on the nationally normed achievement test, to have a focal point for the discussion. As the charts are being passed around the room, these comments are made:

"Wow, look at these test scores for the lowest quintile of fourth graders. You know, most of their parents did not even complete high school!"

"Yes, and I don't want to sound like a racist, but did you notice how many are kids from the East Side of Maple View."

"Well, we are doing a good job with the high achievers."

"I knew our good kids would pull us through."

"The kids at the bottom are doing the best they can. Let's not be too hard on them. If we push them too hard, they'll drop out. What are we supposed to do?

Beatrice returns to her office, deflated. What she had intended as a session in how best to serve the needs of underachieving learners turned into a session in reinforcing stereotypes. At the next meeting, she takes a different approach.

Beatrice starts by saying, "Since our last meeting, I have given a lot of thought to this assignment to look at these data. I think we pursued the wrong path with these charts. Today, I want us to look for trends and patterns in the data and to ask questions of clarification."

"I thought we noted important trends in our first meeting," Joyce says.

"Yes," Brad says, "I thought we clearly pointed out the inadequacies of the children from the East Side, and looked at how well our good students are doing. No surprises anywhere."

Hakim is puzzled. "I left here last time thinking that if we were using these data to inform ourselves about how to better provide for these students, I didn't get it. Dr. Connelly, how do you see today's agenda being any more productive?"

Salwah is thoughtful. "You know, I just completed a class with Dr. Ruth Johnson at the State University, and I learned about the power of looking at these data. How might we use these data to inform our instruction? Is this about us or our students? Dr. Johnson said something has to change! We can't change the kids who come to us. So, that leaves us. What are we willing to do? Dr. Connelly, do you think you could show us a different way to examine these scores?

REFLECT

What issues of cultural precompetence are described in the story? What are the assumptions made by Joyce, Brad, and Hakim? What assumptions are being made by Dr. Connelly and Salway? If you were Dr. Connelly, how would you handle this situation? What would you say to Salwah?

REFLECT

Describe your classroom experiences with behaviors or attitudes that reflect cultural precompetence.

_____

_____

_____

_____

Reflecting on organizations in which you have been employed, describe an organizational policy or practice that illustrates cultural precompetence. Describe a behavior or value of yours or of someone you know that illustrates cultural precompetence.

_____

_____

_____

_____

Cultural Competence

Cultural competence is any policy, practice, or behavior that uses the essential elements of Cultural Proficiency as the standard for the individual or the organization. These essential elements are assessing culture, valuing diversity, managing the dynamics of difference, adapting to diversity, and institutionalizing cultural knowledge. Though these elements are presented here and in the chapters that follow as separate concepts, in practice, they function interactively.

Culturally competent instructors or organizations are students of themselves and of their organizations, either because they purposely set out to study themselves and their organizations or because their personal ethical framework involves their continual observation of themselves and their organizations in seeking to do what they believe is best. These instructors realize that all learners have the capacity to learn and that it is the instructor's responsibility to create an environment in which the learner can use that capacity for learning. In contrast to the story with Dr. Connelly and the precompetent committee, the culturally competent committee would have used the data to ask this key question: What is it that we have to do differently for these children and youths to succeed academically and socially?

Maple View Middle School had recently undergone review by its regional accrediting agency (RAA). A team of fifteen educators spent five days on campus studying the school from every conceivable angle. Their primary documents were the school's self-study responding to the RAA's standards for excellence and many other documents at the school site. In addition, the team made classroom observations and conducted extensive interviews with faculty and staff members, students, community members, parents, and all major advisory and decision-making groups. At the end of their visit, they issued a comprehensive report that, though generally positive, included the disturbing finding that participation in the school's extracurricular activities did not reveal an equitable participation by the various ethnic groups that attended the school.

Central office gave Rose Diaz-Harris, the principal, the task of collecting and disaggregating the data, analyzing it, and making appropriate recommendations. She developed a two-pronged strategy. First, she collected the data from the school's data system and disaggregated it by gender and ethnicity. The patterns she found could only be identified as segregated. In interviewing learners, she found activities that the students indicated as intended for European American students, African American students, Latino students, or Asian Pacific students. Only the student government and the major sports teams were integrated in a fashion that represented the profile of the school.

Second, Rose and a group of instructors used the essential elements of Cultural Proficiency to develop a strategic plan for improving student involvement in the school's extracurricular program. Their overarching goal for the next academic year was to involve sports and activity sponsors in recruiting students from across the campus into the activities. The school faculty decided that the extracurricular program exists to provide students with successful social experiences as an important adjunct to the curricular program of the school. The school administration and faculty now view both the curricular and the extracurricular programs as fundamental to student success. A major part of that success is providing students with the opportunity to develop cross-cultural relationships.

Once the school administrators and faculty members had agreed about their major goals, Rose formed a committee comprising activity sponsors, coaches, and students to review the disaggregated data in light of the goals. Rose makes a short presentation on the essential elements of cultural competence and opens the floor to questions and comments.

Coach Blanford says, "You know, I had noticed that my tennis team was mostly white and Asian students, of course, but I didn't think anything of that. Now, I can see where women might think I was discriminating."

Lucy Simmons responds, "Yeah, you're right. That's the case with the chess club, too. It hadn't occurred to me that we don't recruit students who might want to learn to play chess. Basically, we organize tournaments within members of the club. We might have a different atmosphere if we approached recruiting students who have never played chess before."

"I think what we are talking about is important," says Tom Lee, the student body president. "I often sense tension among racial groups of students on campus. It seems to me that using the extracurricular activities to outreach could promote harmony on campus. It is like in our classes; some teachers provide opportunities for us to work in groups, but most do not. There is a lot of isolation on campus."

"I want to speak as an instructor at this school," says Lou Bono. "I think Rose is on to something here. Ever since the incident at Columbine High School many years ago, two things have haunted me. First is the obvious concern for those who were shot. However, the message that stays with me was the statement by the principal on the opening day of school the next fall. You may have seen it on CNN. He said to the assembled students, faculty, and staff that it was their collective responsibility to involve the students on the edge of the school's culture in the life of the school. If that is not a telling comment, I don't know what is. Not that I think that would necessarily happen here, but just to acknowledge that there are students 'on the edge of the culture' is pretty revealing. I bet that would describe the situation in nearly every school in the country."

REFLECT

What are the issues of cultural competence presented in the story? What assumptions are made by Coach Blanford, Lucy Simmons, Tom Lee, and Lou Bono? If you were Rose, how would you proceed?

_____

_____

_____

_____

REFLECT

Describe your experiences as an instructor with behaviors or attitudes that reflect cultural competence.

_____

_____

_____

_____

Reflecting on organizations in which you have been employed, describe an organizational policy or practice that illustrates cultural competence. Describe a behavior or value of yours or of someone you know that illustrates cultural competence.

_____

_____

_____

_____

Cultural Proficiency

Cultural Proficiency is manifest in organizations and people who esteem culture, who know how to learn about individual and organizational cultures, and who interact effectively with a variety of cultural groups. Cultural Proficiency is not a destination but, rather, a way of being. It is an ongoing and unfolding process as you learn about yourself, your organization, and the people who work with you. To be culturally proficient doesn't mean you know all there is to know about diversity. It means you have learned how to learn. You have learned how to be a student of culture and a cultural informant to others about the cultural expectations of the environments that you do know well.

Janet Miller-Perez, assistant principal at the Middle School, is excited about the school's community engagement program. She has organized African American and Spanish-speaking teams to reach out to prospective African American and Hispanic families to engage in school activities with their students. The Spanish-speaking families have increased their attendance at school events by 70 percent over last year's attendance. The African American families also have increased their participation at all school events, by 82 percent over the past several years. Overall, parents' attendance at school events has increased over 80 percent from last year.

"What we noticed," Janet tells her principal, who had asked to what she credited the increased attendance, "is that all parents do care about their kids. Our Plan for Culturally Proficient Practices includes parents as our partners. We hosted evenings specifically for Spanish-speaking parents to review school procedures and documents with our interpreters here. We hosted An Evening of African American Arts and Culture to engage our community with African American families to help build trust. And, we continued to host Parenting of the Middle Grades student workshops for all parents throughout the year. Of course, our teachers and administrators' home visits have been well received also. These have been huge successes for our parents and for us. We still need to work out how we can be more 'of and in the community' rather than expecting the community to always come to us."

Culturally proficient instructors don't know everything, but they probably know what they need to know, and they know how to ask for help.

REFLECT

Reflecting on organizations in which you have been employed. Describe an organizational policy or practice that illustrates Cultural Proficiency. Describe a behavior or value of yours or of someone you know that illustrates Cultural Proficiency.

_____

_____

_____

_____

GO DEEPER

Think about your classroom and about other classrooms in which you've observed, perhaps as a learner. List a teaching practice or behavior (or an organizational policy or practice) that illustrates each of the six phases along the continuum (see Figure 6.2).

Figure 6.2 Cultural Proficiency Continuum

Reactive Change Mandated for Tolerance			Proactive Change Chosen for Transformation		
Destructiveness	**Incapacity**	**Blindness**	**Precompetence**	**Competence**	**Proficiency**
Eliminate differences. The elimination of other people's cultures	Demean differences. Belief in the superiority of one's culture and behavior that disempowers another's culture	Dismiss differences. Acting as if the cultural differences you see do not matter or not recognizing that there are differences among and between cultures	Respond inadequately to the dynamics of difference. Awareness of the limitations of one's skills or an organization's practices when interacting with other cultural groups	Engage with differences using the essential elements as standards. Using the five essential elements of Cultural Proficiency as the standard for individual behavior and organizational practices	Esteem and learn from differences as a lifelong practice. Knowing how to learn about and from individual and organizational culture; interacting effectively in a variety of cultural environments; advocating for others

Cultural Destructiveness

_____

_____

_____

_____

Cultural Incapacity

_____

_____

_____

_____

Cultural Blindness

_____

_____

_____

Cultural Precompetence

_____

_____

_____

_____

Cultural Competence

_____

_____

_____

_____

Cultural Proficiency

_____

_____

_____

_____

Part III

The Essential Elements

- *Assess Culture:* Identify the cultures present in a system, including organizational cultures.
- *Value Diversity:* Demonstrate an appreciation for the differences among and between groups in policies and practices.
- *Manage the Dynamics of Difference:* Respond appropriately and effectively to the conflicts and issues that arise in a diverse environment.
- *Adapt to Diversity:* Change and adopt policies and practices to support both diversity and inclusion.
- *Institutionalize Cultural Knowledge:* Drive the changes into the organization so they are systemic and systematic.

7 Assessing Culture

To teach students that we are serious about intellectual standards, we must always assess their ability to see the limits of what is learned; they need to have the chance to punch holes in our own or the textbook's presentation. They have a right to demand justification of our point of view. That is what . . . sends the right moral message: we are both student and teacher.

—Grant P. Wiggins[1]

GET CENTERED

What do you know about your own learning style? What do you know about how your own cultural background and experiences affect your learning? Under what conditions do you learn best? How do you respond as a learner when you are asked to do the same task, in the same way, within the same period, using the same materials as other members of the group? Has an instructor ever asked you to describe the best way to teach you? Who is responsible for your learning—you or the instructor?

---

[1]Sennett (2004), p. 102.

- Assessing Culture
- Valuing Diversity
- Managing the Dynamics of Difference
- Adapting to Diversity
- Institutionalizing Cultural Knowledge

THE ESSENTIAL ELEMENTS

In this and the following chapters we discuss the five essential elements of Cultural Proficiency (see Figure 7.1). Each element provides a standard for teaching and learning. The elements can be used for planning change or evaluating it. An understanding of the essential elements will provide you with the behavioral framework for addressing differences and moving toward Cultural Proficiency. Cultural Proficiency is not a tool for addressing diversity; it is a tool for creating an environment where everyone has equitable access to success.

Carol Cheng

Carol Cheng is a ninth-grade teacher at Continuation High School in Maple View School District. She recently moved to Maple View from the nearby metropolitan area, seeking a better job opportunity and affordable housing. Carol is twenty-nine years old and single, and she enjoys sports and recreation. She also places high value on community involvement and enjoys being a member of the Maple View Community Recreation Committee. She is a member of Leadership Maple View, and during her term, she hopes to initiate a project to improve the old park on Avenue A to create a youth development center for sports activities. Carol hopes that by working with the teens on the East Side, she can encourage more students to attend the community college when they graduate from high school. Carol hopes her new projects will help students have access to opportunities that their perceived deficits have denied them.

Carol recently met Al Hernandez, whom she had seen at school district meetings and at her local coffee shop. Carol was pleased to have finally met someone who had similar education and community values. Carol and Rose, Al's wife, also have become good friends, and when the two couples—Al and Rose and Carol and James—get together, they are always talking about their schools and their teaching experiences. James is an instructor at the local community college. He explains to the other three that he teaches, too. "You don't have to have children seated in desks, lined in rows, with books in their hands to be a teacher. My students are adults who have jobs and families, sit at round tables, and discuss their learning goals." James isn't sure the three traditional teachers saw his point.

Carol had recently been asked to assist with professional development for the classified employees' orientation at the district office. She isn't sure why she was selected. Al explains that she was viewed by the district assistant superintendent as an excellent instructor who worked well with everyone and one who "gets" this Cultural Proficiency approach really well.

"Does it have anything to do with the fact that I am Chinese?" Carol laughs.

"Not at all. Well, yes, I mean, no—now you've got me culturally confused." They all laugh nervously.

In this new role Carol is responsible for designing and implementing a training program for classified employees in the areas of conflict resolution, communication, and employee relations. Prior to becoming a teacher at Maple View, Carol's area of study was anthropology and she had specialized in organizational development with a large corporate firm. She was hired to help the organization work through some of its issues of diversity in the workplace. When Al first met Carol, she explained how she had struggled with her identity as an Asian American woman who was often caught between two very different cultural realities. Her grandparents and even her parents sometimes had expectations and values that were different from those that Carol had become accustomed to in Maple View and her former big city environment. Al, Carol, Rose, and James often have conversations about how they view themselves as cultural beings and how others, friends, family, and strangers often have conflicting perceptions of their cultural being. Many persons openly express surprise that the four of them spend so much time together.

Carol confides in Al and her close friends that evening, "I'm looking forward to working with the assistant superintendent to design the professional learning for new teachers. One of the first things I will suggest is that we examine: Who are we and how do we think we are perceived as Maple View employees? That should get the conversation started with assessing our own cultural knowledge!"

Over the past couple of decades, educators and other researchers have written a great deal about learning styles. Thanks to the work of Howard Gardner and others, instructors today, more than ever before in the history of American education, have an opportunity to know a great deal about how individuals learn best. The literature clearly shows that no two learners, or groups of learners, process information in the same way, nor do they read, hear, speak, or think in the same way. The obvious task for instructors is to find out how their students learn best. This task is neither simple nor easy. The process of finding out is called *assessment.*

REFLECT

The learners who enter your classroom have not only their own learning styles but also their own distinctive cultural backgrounds and experiences. As the person in charge of your students' learning, you also bring to the classroom your own distinctive experiences and culture. As a culturally proficient instructor, you understand, appreciate, and respect the various cultures represented in your classroom, and you try to proactively design instructional strategies that include all learners. You also understand the power you possess by virtue of being the instructor, the person *in charge.* How do you approach instruction and learning in your classroom?

_____

_____

_____

_____

Learning Styles and Culturally Proficient Instruction

Culturally proficient instructors are aware of their own learning styles and the learning styles of their students. They also know about their own culture and the effects their culture may have on the other people in the classroom. They realize that instructors play a powerful role in the classroom.

When an instructor walks into the classroom for the first time with a new group or class, she or he is the center of attention. The learners look to see the physical attributes of the instructor: hair color, height, weight, and complexion. They wait to hear the sound of the instructor's voice and the first words spoken. The clothing the instructor wears, accessories and adornments, and the way the instructor looks at them—or doesn't look at them—intrigues the learners. The interaction between learner and instructor begins the moment the instructor enters the room, even before the learners ask the first question or engage in conversation.

Dr. Barbara Carpenter was pleased to be giving the opening comments for the teachers' back-to-school in-service and picnic. She knew that several new instructors would be in the audience and she wanted to make sure that they, as well as the returning teachers and staff members, would leave the opening session having a clear understanding of Cultural Proficiency and of the essential elements of culturally proficient instruction. After her presentation, she asked her colleague Nancy to review her speech and give her feedback.

"The speech was really good," Nancy says. "I like how you spelled out the importance of our teachers taking time to get to know each and every learner. But I was just wondering why you felt it was necessary to tell the audience about your own family reunion last summer. The part about your sister being a doctor and the two of you being raised by your grandmother seems a little 'extra' to me. Is that part of the 'black experience' your people talk about?"

"It's about my experience, and I am black. So by sharing my own story and my family values, instructors may see how important it is to share their cultural and family values with their learners. I hope that what I say will model the inside-out perspective of Cultural Proficiency. We get to know our learners one student at a time, you know. By the way, didn't you recently visit your sister back East? Let's go get a cup of coffee. I want to hear all about your favorite sister."

The culturally proficient instructor understands the powerful effect of culture on what takes place in the classroom. Knowing your own culture and how others interact with you is critical to culturally proficient instruction. Cultural Proficiency's inside-out approach to diversity encourages instructors to understand and acknowledge their own cultures. That is, the essential element "assessing culture" begins with the individual or the organization first assessing her or his or its own culture. With this self-assessment comes a greater appreciation of how diverse learners interact with you the instructor.

Ralph, an eighth-grade teacher, was preparing for his first day in his own classroom at Pine View Middle School. The bulletin boards were ready. The class roster was complete. Textbooks were on the shelves. Ralph walks down the hallway to ask his mentor teacher, Charlene Brennaman, one final question: "Charlene, how will I know how to teach them?"

"Teach them the way they learn best."

"How will I know how they learn best?"

"Ask them. They will tell you, and they will show you how to teach them. All you have to do is ask." Then, she pauses, turns back to him, and adds, "And ask often."

So how do you become aware of and knowledgeable about how the learners in your classroom learn best? A starting point is for you to know how you, yourself, learn best. As an adult learner, you probably have not been asked recently to think about your own learning. Intuitively, many of us go about our routines of reading, writing, speaking, and listening in ways that are most comfortable to us.

Think of the conflict—or the comedy—that might erupt if parents and children sat down at the breakfast table and took turns reading the morning newspaper aloud, followed by a brief quiz on the content. Funny as it may seem, isn't that what instructors sometimes ask classrooms of thirty learners to do? Isn't the process similar when a personnel director hands out a procedures manual to fourteen new employees and says, "Take ten minutes and silently read Pages 2 through 7, then I'll give you a quiz to see whether you know the correct procedures"?

At the breakfast table, many parents encourage discussion of issues that individual family members have read in the paper or heard on the news. An alternative for the personnel director might be to allow each of the new employees time to read, ask questions, and think about the assigned section in the procedures manual before administering the quiz. Instead, the director might ask the employees to perform the required task rather than to write about it. These strategies create a safer, less threatening learning environment and take into consideration students' differences in learning styles.

BECOMING AWARE OF EACH LEARNER'S UNIQUENESS

Imagine for a moment that you are standing on the shoreline of an Alaskan city looking out over the vast inland waterway filled with massive icebergs. Each iceberg floats independently, but the collection of the icebergs offers an even more impressive scene. As you stand in awe of the magnificence of the iceberg field, a friend standing nearby offers you a pair of special binoculars so that you can actually see below the surface of the water. You are a bit skeptical, at first, but you trust your friend's innovative ideas, so you take the special binoculars and hold them to your eyes. To your amazement, you can now see what you only suspected moments before. Below the surface is the gigantic outline of one of the icebergs. It plunges deep below the surface and has features unlike the ice that protrudes above the surface. You can see the detail of the ice formation and the texture and hues that you could not see when your view was confined to the surface. Then, still looking through the binoculars, you notice something even more profound. Each iceberg is unique. Some have sharp, craggy edges; others appear smoother, almost glasslike. As many icebergs as there are floating in the waterway, there are as many different appearances to the shapes and sizes of each iceberg. Each one is unique in its own design.

Reluctantly, you return the special glasses to your friend. You are somewhat sad because you would like to keep the glasses so you could always see the uniqueness of the icebergs. Your friend takes the glasses and says, "Now that you have seen below the surface, you'll never look at them the same way again. You won't need the special glasses anymore. You are special because of what you see now."

Just as you could see the unique aspects of icebergs even after removing your special glasses, you will be able to see the unique aspects of your learners after you finish reading this book on Cultural Proficiency. Once you have learned how to be sensitive to your students' distinctive cultural backgrounds, experiences, and learning styles, you will view them this way without the aid of your "special glasses." The essential elements of Cultural Proficiency will serve as your special glasses for recognizing each student's unique individuality and distinctive cultural background. Each classroom of learners will present you with a new opportunity to see each learner's uniqueness. Your special sensitivity will enhance your instruction and facilitate your students' learning. Your knowledge of cultures and of learning styles will help you and the learners in the complex cognitive process of learning.

In addition to gaining understanding of your students' cultures, you will enhance your instruction by assessing your own culture and the organizational culture in which you work and teach. As a culturally proficient instructor, you will assess the impact of your own culture on your instructional behaviors. You will see that your preferences for instructional strategies may be grounded in your own learning style rather than in the style best suited to your learners. As a culturally proficient instructor, you will know and appreciate the complexity and importance of the diverse cultures in your classroom or training program. You will realize the impact of your own attitudes, habits, feelings, and actions on your students or trainees. You also will demonstrate a variety of instructional strategies that respect and support the various cultures of the learners you teach.

REFLECT

Do you recall an experience when the learners reacted negatively to you as an instructor? Were they reacting to you as a person, to the lesson itself, or to the situational context of the learning? What did you do in response to the negative behavior?

_____

_____

_____

_____

If you answered no to the first question, do you know why learners have always reacted to you in a positive way? Who are the learners? Who are you in the presence of the learners? What difference does your approach make in how learners respond to you?

_____

_____

_____

_____

ASSESSING INDIVIDUAL CULTURE

Culturally proficient instructors are aware of their own culture. As a culturally proficient instructor, you also are aware that your culture acts on and through your instructional behaviors in the classroom. A brief self-assessment using the following questions can guide you to a deeper understanding of the relationship between knowing your culture and choosing appropriate instructional strategies.

ENGAGE

Discuss your answers to these questions with your colleagues.

- What do you know about your own name?
- How does it reflect your cultural heritage?
- How does your name reflect your family's history?
- How does it reflect your personal history?
- What does your name mean?
- What is the story of how you acquired your name?
- Have you had any other names?

- How do people respond when they see or hear your name for the first time?
- If you changed your name what would it be?

Have you thought about your entrance into the classroom of new learners? What happens when you walk into the classroom for the first time? Have you ever noticed how the learners respond?

_____

_____

_____

REFLECT

How do you describe your culture?

_____

_____

_____

Do you wait to describe your culture until a member of the class asks you about it, or do you share aspects of your culture as part of the classroom instruction?

_____

_____

_____

In addition to instructional time, what opportunities do you have to share with your students some information about your culture?

_____

_____

_____

Have you noticed that learners of your culture react and relate to you in different ways than do learners from cultures that differ from yours?

_____

_____

_____

REFLECT

Who are you? What do you want others to know about you as a person, an instructor, and a learner? Take a few minutes to write your own story.

_____

_____

_____

_____

In addition to assessing your own culture, you will be involved in helping others to assess their own cultures. In the following story, the instructor fails to elicit the responses she seeks from her trainees. As you read the story, think about how you might have handled the situation differently.

> Carol Song is beginning the first day of diversity training for all classified employees of Maple View School District. She has asked the group to respond to a question during an opening learning strategy: "Introduce yourself by giving your name, your cultural background, and any specialized training that you have had."
>
> Harland, one of the participants, protests. "I'm American. I don't have a culture like you do. What am I supposed to say? How do I describe my culture, except to say that I am white and I'm American? Don't you have to be from somewhere else, a minority, to really have a culture?"

Neither Carol, the trainer, nor the other participants were aware of the impact Carol's opening question would have on different members of the group. Harland responded defensively, assuming that because the training was about diversity, the question was intended for people of color, thereby excluding white people from having "culture." Carol, however, had hoped the question would allow each person in the group to describe his or her cultural background, regardless of ethnicity. She had hoped also that knowing the culture of others would help the members of the group respect and appreciate each other.

Carol had assumed that all the people in the group knew their cultural backgrounds and would be willing to openly share that information. She also assumed that everyone already agreed with one of her deeply held beliefs: Acknowledging our cultural differences and similarities is an effective way for a group of employees to work and learn together. By failing to realize that not all employees shared her belief at the start of the training, she prompted stronger resistance to the training from the participants.

Perhaps Carol's opening comments could have been more descriptive:

"Culture is everything you believe and do that identifies you as a part of a group and distinguishes you from other groups. Most people think of culture as their race or ethnicity, but we are much more complex than that. Most people belong to several groups and identify strongly with two or three. So when I ask you to talk about your culture, I am asking you to think about the groups you identify with or from which you derive your identity. I'd like each of you to tell a little about your cultural background. Perhaps you'd like to start with your name.

"Probably one of the most treasured possessions that we have is our name. Think of your own name and what it means to you and your family. Share with one other person in the room what your name is, what your name means, how your name was chosen, or any interesting story or information about your name. After about five minutes for each of you to talk about your own name, I will ask that you introduce your partner to the rest of the group. I'll invite you to tell a story about your partner's name."

REFLECT

What is your reaction to the preceding introductory comments? Write and rehearse your own script, describing the purpose of knowing one's own culture, as well as the culture of the learners.

_____

_____

_____

_____

ASSESSING ORGANIZATIONAL CULTURE

Thus far, we have noted that culturally proficient instructors assess their own culture, come to understand their students' cultures, and help their students assess their own cultures. In addition, they assess the organizational culture of the environments in which they teach. Organizations have cultures, and each member of the organization functions within the organizational culture. To be effective and successful within an organization, you must assess its organizational culture and learn how to behave appropriately within it. This assessment and awareness of organizational culture helps you to know what behaviors are expected and affirmed within the organization.

REFLECT

Think of a time when you violated one of the unwritten rules of your school or company. How did you know you had broken the rule? How were you expected to have known the rule? How do you learn the cultural expectations of an organization?

_____

_____

_____

_____

By knowing about and understanding the culture of the organization in which you work, you will be better able to interact with learners, confront conflict with colleagues, and enhance your organizational relationships and communication. As a culturally proficient instructor, you will work toward establishing the cultural norms within your organization. You will help to determine those norms after assessing the values and beliefs held by members of the organization. You will recognize that these norms must reflect working agreements shared by the organizations' members. Once these cultural norms are established, you will ensure that they are stated explicitly and shared by leaders and workers throughout the organization.

It is important for members of the organization to know and assess how others—both inside and outside the organization—perceive the organization. Most people learn an organization's culture intuitively. When you are working with a diverse group of people, they may not have the cultural background to intuit the cultural norms of your particular organization. A culturally proficient instructor articulates the organization's cultural expectations to all learners. At times, it may be useful to evaluate your organizational culture by using an assessment instrument as a tool to analyze and understand the impact of this culture on instruction and learning. The results of the assessment can then guide you in adjusting your presentation style, in selecting materials, and in determining your instructional strategies.

Meet Carlos Montanaro

Carlos Montanaro, HR Director of the Maple View School District, meets with all new employees to give them a tour of the school district on their first day on the job. He gives each new employee a school district logo lapel pin, a logo writing pen, and a framed district logo vision and mission statement. He begins the tour in the district office at his office desk and by looking at photos of his father, one of the first employees of the district forty-five years ago. His father was a custodian.

His typical welcome speech is: "I am pleased and proud to welcome you to our district. We are a family here. You might say this is my family's business. As you can see in these pictures, my father was a hard-working man who worked right along with other early employees here. I do the same thing. You will see me in the school yards or here in the central office or out in the community. I will always be where the work and the workers are."

One day, a new employee says to Carlos, "I'm glad to be here. I do have a few questions, though. I also heard that you help folks get started again with their education or training. I want finish my master's degree and receive additional professional development. Does the district support additional education? And one more thing, I don't speak Spanish or any language other than English. Is that a problem? I noticed that a lot of the teachers here do speak Spanish."

Carlos responds, "We believe in being lifelong learners here at Maple View. And, about being Spanish-speaking, we appreciate our workers here for what they know and what they are willing to learn. Just ask for help when you need it. Welcome to Maple View and welcome to the family."

REFLECT

Think about the organization in which you work. Is the organization as a whole supportive of instruction and learning? Do members of the organization affirm and value employees from diverse cultures?

_____

_____

_____

_____

_____

Think of a time when you were a member of a planning team for an employee workshop or training session. What role did your culture or ethnicity play in the planning process? Were cultural differences topics of discussion in the planning sessions? Did the planning team make efforts to respect and allow for cultural differences of the trainers and the learners? How did the conversation about individual differences sound to you? As a culturally proficient instructor, how could you frame the next planning session to include norms for Cultural Proficiency?

It is important for instructors to know and assess how others, both inside and outside the organization, perceive the organization. Those outside the organization behave in ways that are consistent with their perceptions of how the organization treats its employees, its learners, and its community. Often, members of a community will avoid calling the school or coming to the school if they have heard that the teachers don't value parent involvement. Community members avoid working with certain agencies when they perceive that the agency does not value diversity. When the employees of an organization treat people outside the organization in ways that are demeaning and disrespectful, the outside community views the organization itself in the same way. By assessing this perception, the culturally proficient instructor is better able to understand why members of the learning community react negatively to members of the organization.

Carlos Montanaro's wife, Anita, is president of the Pine Hills High School PTA. Members of the community often ask her and Carlos questions about the high school. Both Carlos and Anita are very active in community and volunteer organizations throughout the city and have served on the city's leadership committee.

At a leadership committee meeting, Lupe, a member of the committee, asks Anita: "I have been meaning to ask you about the afterschool tutoring at the high school. Does your son Tony go to any of the sessions? We want Roberto to go, but he says he is not eligible to stay after school because he has to ride the bus home. What should I do to get him some help?"

"Oh, I think the school has a learning strategy bus that takes kids home after the tutoring classes. Just call the school and ask someone there to give you the information."

"I don't like to call the school," Lupe confesses. "My English is not very good, and I don't think they like it when I call. I always feel like I am causing them too much trouble. Besides, the learning strategy bus only drops kids off on the West Side. They said it was too far and there were too many kids to drop off on the East Side where we live."

Anita sympathizes. "I'm sorry you have not been well received at the school, Lupe. I'll mention your concerns to the school principal and to the PTA leadership council. We should all be working on these issues together."

GO DEEPER

What have you learned from the stories in this chapter? What have you learned about yourself? What have you learned about the organization in which you work? Observe yourself over the next few weeks. How and what do you share about your values and your beliefs with the people you teach? What do you do to learn about the people in your classroom? How does that inform and influence what and how you teach?

_____

_____

_____

_____

8 Valuing Diversity

America is the most diverse country in the history of the world. How are we dealing with diversity. . .? Standardization.

—Paul D. Houston[1]

Think of your closest friends. List their names on paper or close your eyes and imagine them. Now think about what it is that you like about them. What do they have in common that you like? What are the unique characteristics they possess? As you think about their characteristics, what does this tell you about what you value in friendships?

_____

_____

_____

_____

- ■ Assessing Culture
- ■ Valuing Diversity
- ▨ Managing the Dynamics of Difference
- ▨ Adapting to Diversity
- ▨ Institutionalizing Cultural Knowledge

---

[1]Sennett (2004), p. 23.

Helen Williams

Maple View School District has many outstanding employees. Al Hernandez considers Helen Williams to be someone who is well grounded and very plain spoken. He wonders what she might say about teaching and living in Maple View. He remembers that she has lived and worked in the community for many years and is well thought of by other teachers in the district. Al decides to visit Helen in her classroom one afternoon after school. Helen is an African American preschool teacher in her early 60s, who has been teaching preschool children in Maple View "all her life." When Al asks her how long she had been teaching in the district, Helen responds, "I moved here with my family when I was only five years old. My father was the minister at the East Side Methodist Church for fifteen years before he retired and moved back to his home in Louisiana. My mother was the head librarian at Maple View Public Library until she died, two years before my dad's retirement."

Helen and her husband, Leonard, have lived in the same house on Avenue B for the past forty-two years. Leonard is the day manager and dispatcher at MedSupplies.com. He transferred to the company after working twenty years at the parent company, Med Supplies and Equipment Co., in a nearby city. Helen is pleased that "the company treats Leonard well. He is one of their most loyal employees. The transfer was a promotion for him and a way to get him closer to home for his last five years with the company."

Helen has decided not to retire until she absolutely has to. "These preschool children have been my children," she says, "and I'm not leaving them anytime soon." From time to time, Helen and Leonard have taken in foster children as their way of parenting children who needed their love. Helen was honored as Maple View's 1995 Outstanding Citizen of the Year for her leadership in working with at-risk children in the community.

"Every morning of the school year for the past forty-two years, I have walked the two blocks from my home on Avenue B to this classroom at Maple View Elementary School." Helen chronicles her story for Al. For the past twenty years, not only has Helen taught her classes, but she also has coordinated the school's Head Start program and English learners program. The principal at the school recently talked to Helen about some of the mandated changes in the programs at the school and requested that Helen go for some training at the district office to better understand some new opportunities for funding support for the preschool. Helen is excited that the principal asked her to go for the training because the younger teachers "just don't understand what these children need."

Al asks Helen what she thought about the recent letters to the editor and the editorial about the so-called East Side story. "What's so secret about the story? The families on this side of town know what's happening. It's no secret over here. Many people do not see and, therefore, don't value the customs and other life realities of our community. We are invisible to most of the people on the West Side. Go talk to some of the teachers over there and let them tell you how it looks from their point of view."

Al decides to do just that.

Valuing is something people do naturally. You express your values all the time. All people do. You decided to be an instructor because you value learning. You picked up this book because you were interested in the topic, and you probably have continued to read this book because you value what you are reading.

People find valued similarities among their friends—such as their intelligence, sense of humor, compassion, or sense of adventure. Among your friends you also may find differences that you value as well. One friend collects and repairs vintage automobiles. In her, you value how she focuses on an avocation. Another friend is confident in speaking out on social issues. In him, you value his commitment to his ideals. You may, or may not, invite all these people to the same dinner party, but they are your close friends just the same. The key element is that you value your friendships with these people, with their similarities and their differences. You value their diversity.

Diversity is as ever-present as the air we breathe. To ask, "Do you believe in diversity?" is tantamount to asking, "Do you believe in the sun?" Diversity is not something to believe in. It exists. Look around you and see diversity everywhere you turn.

What creates a conflict for some is the need to say, "Yes I see diversity, but shouldn't we emphasize our similarities?" We respond, "Not necessarily. It is important to recognize the differences and to notice the differences that make a difference. Only then is it effective for an instructor to focus on similarities."

If you focused solely on similarities when you were teaching, you would be focusing only on the lowest common denominator among your learners. Just as you value the similarities and differences in your friends, you can appreciate that difference and similarity balance each other—the *yin* and *yang* of human existence. As a culturally proficient instructor, you look among the learners in your classroom and see both their similarities and their differences. You note the similarities and notice also the differences that make a difference.

REFLECT

What is the nature of the diversity in your current professional setting? How would you describe it to someone who is visiting your classroom setting?

_____

_____

_____

_____

AN INTENTIONAL ACT

In this book, we often allude to the *principle of intentionality*. When you proceed with the conscious intention of doing something differently, you increase the likelihood of achieving your desired outcome. To act with intention is to behave with clear awareness of your goals and intentions and to keep those intentions in your consciousness as you go about your work. For example, if you intend to be a culturally proficient instructor, you may think about some particular changes in attitude and behavior that you want to focus on right now. Each time you walk into your classroom or training room, you remind yourself of your intention to be culturally proficient. Then, you pay careful attention to the specific behaviors that you are focusing on today.

To value diversity is to teach with the intention of valuing diversity and to pay attention to those things that reflect diversity in your classroom. As an instructor who values diversity, you foster a learning community, recognizing that diversity is always present in your classroom, even when such diversity is not strongly evident. You organize your classroom so that materials, instructional delivery systems, and patterns of attention to learners fully acknowledge diversity. You value the diverse classroom as an opportunity to enhance your teaching and learning. You motivate students to learn, and you encourage learners to engage in the content, learn from one another, and develop healthy attitudes about society. You are informed by your teaching, continually learning and applying new strategies for learning. When viewed as a whole, your behaviors illustrate that you value diversity, revealing your commitment to the learning community. In valuing diversity, you see opportunities to learn from your students and your colleagues.

To value diversity is to be clear about what you and your organization perceive to be important. It is nearly impossible to enter an organization today—school or corporate office—and not encounter its mission, vision, or core values statement displayed prominently. These statements almost always describe a value for diversity within the organization and in the community it serves. Such statements have meaning when they truly reflect the core values of the organization and the shared values of the people within it. In reality, these statements are often written by small committees to satisfy an external accreditation agency and thus do not reflect how employees or constituent groups are valued or treated. In order to determine the values of the person or organization, one also must observe a person's behavior or an organization's practices. Values are reflected in what one says and does.

REFLECT

Read the following questions, one at a time, then think; don't write, just think about your response. Then, go to the next question until you have read them all.

- Have you ever been in a situation in which a new employee entered your organization and you wondered whether she or he was an affirmative action hire?
- Have you been in a situation in which you wondered whether a person who spoke slowly and deliberately was very intelligent?
- Have you ever been in a setting in which one person spoke limited English and those around her or him spoke more loudly so the person could understand?

- Have you ever been in a situation in which you felt uncomfortable because you were noticeably different from others in the group?
- Does your organization honor some holidays but not yours?
- Does your organization have a mission statement that includes reaching out into the varied constituent communities it serves but, as a practical matter, serves one primary community?

Now, record your reactions to the questions. Do not answer the questions, just focus on how you felt as you read the questions. Your response will aid you in continuing to clarify your understanding of what it means to value diversity.

_____

_____

_____

_____

In each of the foregoing situations, an organization or the people in it considered but did not value differences. Culturally proficient instructors use specific diversity-valuing behaviors in the classroom and with colleagues. For one thing, they frame the conversation about learners around the differences that make a difference, and they pay attention to how to provide an effective learning environment for their diverse learners.

Maple View Elementary School is in the first of a three-year educational reform process. Following directives from the state and guidance from the school district, the school has been examining disaggregated test data to inform the reform process. The state's department of education disaggregated reading, mathematics, and writing data from a widely used norm-referenced test in order for educators and community members to examine the demographic groups within each school.

Based on these test data, educators have concluded that children from low-income families are not performing nearly as well as they should. This is disproportionately the case for students who are African American, Latino, Native American, and Southeast Asian. Maple View Elementary School has formed an Educator-Parent-Business and Community Team (EPBaCT) to guide the development of an improvement plan. The EPBaCT has conducted input sessions with parents and other members of the community, as well as with teachers and counselors, to gauge their perceptions of what is working well in the school and of what improvements are needed. The input sessions focused on curricular issues (e.g., reading, mathematics, and English language learning) and school climate issues (e.g., safety, discipline patterns, role of parents). Those data have been studied, categorized, and readied for alignment with test scores.

At this evening's meeting, the test data are being distributed for the first time. The twelve members of the EPBaCT are in attendance, and the facilitator from the district office is distributing the data. The data sheets summarize reading, mathematics, and writing results for the previous year's second-, fourth-, and sixth-grade students. The data are summarized by grade level and are disaggregated by gender and ethnicity. The data are then further disaggregated into five quintiles (i.e., each band of 20 percent of students: 1 to 20 percent; 21 to 40 percent, etc.). Accompanying the data sheets are demographic profiles of the families of students at the school. A profile of parents' ethnicity and of the number of years the students attended school is included. As the data sheets were being distributed, Karl says, "Wow! This is a ton of data. How will we ever make sense of this?"

"I don't know," Helen Williams replies, "but I am sure our facilitator will guide us as well as she did with the data from the input sessions."

Helen then hears one parent, Carolyn, comment to another, "Gosh, look at the levels of school completion by our parents! Nearly 62 percent of our parents have not gone beyond eighth grade. No wonder these test scores are so low!"

"You know," Helen says gently to Carolyn, "I hope we don't build obstacles for our children. It's our responsibility as educators to work with all children to attain high achievement levels."

The facilitator then addresses the group: "This side conversation is raising an extremely important point. Either we can use these data to stereotype our children or we can use them to identify areas where we need to do things differently at the school. We have the choice—either we believe that children have the capacity to learn or we build artificial barriers for them."

Carolyn says, "I must say, this is an astonishing approach. Ten years ago I was on one of these committees when our oldest child was at this school and the approach then was that given our demographics the children were doing pretty well."

"Yes," Karl responds, "educators have begun to see that the choice is ours. We can blame the child's neighborhood, parents, culture, et cetera for underachievement, or we can accept no excuses and find out how to teach the children."

Helen says, "Yes, we've said for years that we believe all children can learn. We have to ask now, do we believe we can teach all children?"

REFLECT

How are conversations about learners framed where you work? Do you and your colleagues talk in terms of enabling learners? Does the conversation ever shift to external reasons why they don't learn (e.g., culture, socioeconomic status, or level of education)? Think back to a time when you were engaged in conversation with colleagues that focused on why learners were not performing well. Was the focus on the time that the learners were not in the classroom (e.g., sociocultural influences) or was the focus on the time spent with the instructors? Do you tend to gravitate to those things over which you have minimal control or influence or to those that are in your sphere of influence? In other words, are you taking control of the situation or are you giving up your power?

_____

_____

_____

_____

ENGAGE

In the space provided here, write a list showing what you have heard people say to explain why learners are not performing well. Next, write a corresponding list indicating what happens when you take control and assume responsibility for learner performance.

_____

_____

_____

_____

Why don't learners perform well? What happens when I assume responsibility for learner performance? What is your emotional response to these two lists?

_____

_____

_____

_____

A SIGN OF RESPECT

To value diversity is to respect the learners and to encourage them to show respect to one another. As a culturally proficient instructor, you treat learners in ways that the learners perceive as respectful. This may mean using a different criterion for respect than you would for yourself, as well as explaining the difference to the learners.

A small group of parents contacted Howard Bridges, principal of West Side High School, and wanted to talk with him about reported insensitivities from a few teachers. Apparently, the teachers are having difficulty pronouncing new students' names and would ask them "What do they call you for short?" or "What do they call you at home?" or "What is your American name?" Howard agrees the issue needs to be addressed—now. He invites his longtime friend, Al Hernandez, to meet with the parents and him.

Howard begins, "I want to thank you so much for bringing this issue to our attention."

Al adds, "I want you to know how shocked we are to hear your concerns, Mr. Flores and Mrs. Kim. While I have never personally heard of this happening, I can imagine it happening. I can also imagine that the teachers are oblivious to how their comments are received."

"Let me say how pleased I am by your responsiveness," Mrs. Kim says. "However, let me begin by saying that I am perfectly comfortable being addressed by my first name, Suzy, and I truly appreciate your consideration in addressing me as you have. Yes, this is an issue that, while not intentional, leaves children feeling devalued. What makes it even more complicated is that some children and their parents adopt American names to make it easier for others."

"Yes," Al says, "but it seems to me that if we take the time to learn how to pronounce someone's name that we are honoring that person and her or his heritage."

"Agreed," Howard says enthusiastically. "I think that it demonstrates our willingness and ability to learn. Let me assure you, we are willing to learn and look to you and other parents in our community to assist us and be our co-learners."

The meeting ends on a very cooperative tone.

After the parents leave, Al says to Howard, "I appreciate your viewpoints. You were truly listening to the parents' point of view. Also, as educators come to know the students, they may well be invited to use other, more familiar names."

"That is a key point. One should be invited to do so." Howard says, "How do you think our colleagues at the high school would react to our raising this issue? What is the best way of doing it?"

"Well, there will be resistance by a few. A presenter last year said that we are still acting as if we are teaching the students who were here a generation ago. This sounds like confirmation of that observation. If it's OK with the two of you, I am going to raise this with our staff development committee. I know we can approach this issue in ways that work for school personnel, as well as for members of our community."

REFLECT

Think back to your most recent experience as a learner. It may have been a professional development session, a college class, or some other setting. How did you experience the way the instructor treated the learners? Did you see instances of disregard? Instances of respect? How do you imagine that learning was affected by this treatment? Can you recall an event in your schooling in which you were treated with disrespect by an instructor? Can you remember the experience? Can you remember your feelings? Are you surprised by how vividly you remember the event and your feelings?

Now, think of an instructor who was quite the opposite. Have you observed an instructor who demonstrated regard for learners, independent of their gender, race, ethnicity, or social class? Describe the learning environment in this scenario.

Take a few moments to look at a current group of learners with whom you are working. Note the areas where you are showing regard for learners and areas in which you would like to improve.

_____

_____

_____

_____

_____

Alicia Alvarez and Rose Diaz-Harris serve on the site council for Maple View Middle School. They are discussing the previous day's site-council meeting, which Rose couldn't attend because she chose to attend an open house at her daughter Susan's school. The teachers at the meeting decided that they wanted to start making home visits to establish rapport with a wider group of parents.

Alicia has mixed feelings about the meeting. On the one hand, she is truly pleased by the teachers' decision. However, she was dismayed by the comments that were made after the announcement. She had heard them say, "Should we dress down? Are the parents going to be embarrassed by having us in their homes? Do we have to eat the food if they offer it?" Alicia felt stunned and embarrassed to hear these comments.

Alicia begins, "Really, Rose, I'm not interested in complaining about the teachers, but the comments surprised and hurt me. These are my neighbors and our children they were describing."

"Oh, I can see why you are disturbed!" Rose says. "Did any of the people appear to be angry about going? Did you detect any underlying negative feelings?"

"No, that's what is so perplexing. They seemed to be genuinely interested in making the home visits. Now I am afraid they will just make things worse."

"I wish I could have been there," Rose says. "The last thing we want to do is to create a schism between any parents and educators at this school. What I have to do is to get on the agenda for both the site council and the next staff meeting to discuss how we enter people's homes, as their guests. As instructors, our role in this activity is to build bridges. We have to act with that intention, and we have to pay attention to everything we say and do. These kinds of insensitive comments can create insurmountable divisions."

REFLECT

Think of a time in your life, professional or personal, when a person made a comment that surprised you and hurt your feelings. Briefly describe the situation and your feelings at the time.

_____

_____

_____

_____

As an instructor, you learn to continuously monitor your teaching. You gain insight into which parts of the curriculum work and which do not. You learn what works for some learners but not for others. Likewise, as a culturally proficient instructor, when you monitor the language you use, try to detect negative judgments that hide just below the surface. These judgments may reflect your unwitting engagement in cultural incapacity. What makes these judgments powerful is that you may not be aware of what you are doing, and your judgments may be experienced as microaggressions. This is why Cultural Proficiency requires both intention and attention.

_____

_____

_____

_____

COLLABORATION

To value diversity is to collaborate. Through collaboration, you show that you value the input and concerns of all the stakeholders in your instructional setting. You recognize the value in considering more than one option, and you establish a precedent for supporting more than one approach to reaching a goal. As a culturally proficient instructor, you continuously monitor your learners' progress as a guide to your teaching, and you organize instruction to help the learners become a community of learners.

One experience that most schools and human service agencies have at regular intervals is accreditation by professional and governmental agencies. When done well, these visits can provide educators with data with which to make effective decisions about their organization. These decisions may involve better serving a constituent group, implementing technology to facilitate services, or making long-range plans for staffing needs.

At Pine Hills High School, one of the accreditation guidelines is to disaggregate the data by gender, ethnicity, and social class (based on free and reduced-cost lunch counts). Al Hernandez has been collecting, arraying, and analyzing data for the high school's upcoming regional accreditation visit. EPBaCT, the school/community team, suggested doing the same for extracurricular activities. When first arrayed, the data showed that students' participation correlated quite highly with their respective numbers in the student body. However, when the disaggregated data was by gender and ethnicity, the result was very interesting.

Addressing the EPBaCT Committee, Al says, "Let me draw your attention to Chart 1. In this chart, you will note that the participation rates for male and female students are comparable to their populations in school. Then, when you look at the next row, you will note that the participation rate of students when arrayed by ethnicity also shows a participation rate across groups comparable to their representation in the school."

Carolyn, a parent, exclaims, "Wow! This is great. Both the school and the accrediting agency should love this."

"Yes, both should," Al says.

David, another parent asks, "But what about our request at the last session to break it down by activities. How did that turn out?"

"Good question," Al says. "Please turn to Chart 2 on the next page. In this chart, you will see that some activities are definitely 'male' and some are definitely 'female.' Now part of that may be easily explained. However, when you look further, by ethnicity, you will find that some activities involve a high percentage of European American, African American, Latino and Latina, or Asian Pacific students. Note also that a few extracurricular activities are well integrated. Chart 3 extends the analysis to show that students from lower-income families participate very little in school activities."

Paulo, one of the students, feigned a laugh. "You didn't need to do a study to find this out. Any student on campus could have told you this."

"The student's right!" Al says. "But if we had not had this opportunity to sit down and take this data-driven look at our school, we may have continued to ignore what is so apparent to our students. If there is a value to this team, it's this kind of collaboration."

Then Carolyn says, "Like we did with the norm-referenced data, our best strategy is to make observations and ask questions about the data so we can seek ways to improve participation. Is that right?"

David and Al both respond, "That's what I want."

"I want to add," Al says, "that this is not about blaming anyone for what we have here. It's about finding ways for all students to be successful at this high school."

REFLECT

Remember a time when you organized your class to do group work and the learners were able to solve a complex problem or do a complicated task. What happened? Do you remember the energy level rising? What were some of the moments of frustration? What else did you observe about the interactions?

_____

_____

_____

_____

VALUING DIFFERENCE

Noticing, appreciating, and respecting differences are fundamental to valuing diversity. In your own classroom, you can see differences and similarities expressed and accepted as equally important aspects of everyone's learning.

Dr. Diana Johnson has been overseeing the implementation of the diversity workshops for employees of the Maple View School District. She worked with the Diversity Staff Development Committee to develop criteria for the selection of consultants. Principally, they wanted consultants who could help the employees be more responsive to the various cultures represented in the classrooms and community. Secondarily, they wanted consultants to initiate activities that would influence the development of more inclusive curricula.

At one of the diversity workshops sponsored by the district, the consultant had posted around the training room posters with these headings: "African American Men," "African American Women," "Latinos," "Latinas," "White Men," "White Women," "Gay Men," and "Lesbians," among others. Participants were invited to take packets of sticky notes and to mill around the room, writing and affixing to the posters the notes on which they had written stereotypes they had heard about the respective groups.

Following the workshop, Howard, an African American high school teacher, was so upset about the activity that he made an appointment to speak with Dr. Johnson. Howard was deeply troubled that differences and similarities can be expressed and accepted as two equally important parts of all people's learning. During their meeting, Howard objected strenuously to comparing stereotypes of African Americans with those of gay men and lesbians.

"Dr. Johnson," Howard begins, "I do not want to participate in diversity activities that seek to compare the experiences of all groups as if they are equal."

Kathryn, one of the teacher participants, says to Howard: "I heard the consultant trying to draw comparisons to stereotypes and the negative effects of stereotypes. I didn't see her trying to make experiences the same."

"Well, I did, and I'm not going to stand for it!" Howard is adamant.

"Howard, do you mean to tell me that as a high school teacher, you're going to engage in a type of *Oppression Olympics*? Though we have had different histories, the object of this activity to keep us from doing to others what has been done to us. In my mind, that does not keep us from knowing and studying our various historical and current experiences. I would think that a good teacher like you would want your students to know the unique experiences of other groups, as well as how those experiences compare across history."

"You have a point," Howard says. "I didn't hear it that way yesterday. It's too bad that consultant didn't express it as clearly as you just did."

"The example I just gave you is the same one she gave you yesterday. You couldn't hear it from her, but you can now from me. Why do you think you can hear it now?"

"To be honest?"

"Of course."

"I thought she was running her own agenda!"

"Howard, over the many years that you have been a teacher, how often have you heard that same allegation made about us?"

"Aaarrrggghhh. I hear you! I guess I have to avoid getting into the trap of thinking that similarities and differences are opposites. They can, and do, exist in our lives at the same time."

REFLECT

Remember a time when someone judged the way you did a task and did not inquire about why you did it that way. Think of a time when you experienced something as different and immediately judged it harshly instead of acknowledging it as a manifestation of diversity. Think of insights you have made about learners in your classrooms when you discovered something about them that you initially judged negatively, only to find that it illustrated how they approached learning differently than you had expected. In the space provided, record your reactions and how you would like to have seen the situation handled differently.

To value diversity is to recognize that each culture finds some values more important than others. As a culturally proficient instructor, you know that some learners value getting the right answer, whereas others want to know how the answer was derived. You recognize that some learners prefer to work alone, while others prefer to work in pairs or in groups.

Pine Hills Elementary School had been experiencing a small immigration of Latino students from Central American countries. Joaquin Jarrin, a sixth-grade teacher there, had a parent conference that left him confused. He had asked for the conference with the parents of his student Josefina to try to determine why she was doing so poorly on a literature and history project. All year long, she had been one of his best students, and her work on this project was clearly below her potential. The conference left him puzzled, so he asked Eduardo Gonzales, one of the third-grade teachers at Maple View Elementary School, to help him sort out what had happened.

"Ed, I am totally confused. Josefina has done exceptionally well all year, until this project. In talking with her parents, all I could discern was that Josefina would not be writing anything that would criticize others."

"What was the project, Joaquin?"

"It's one I have done for several years. I provide the students with source material that offers different perspectives on a historical event. Using the literature of the day, and a rubric, they are to critique the various perspectives. What I want them to learn to analyze and critique these kinds of data."

"Ah, that may be the issue. In some cultures, it is considered presumptuous, even rude, to criticize material provided by the school."

"That's interesting, Ed. I didn't know that. So, I have to teach that critiquing and criticizing are not necessarily the same. In fact, I have to help Josefina and her parents to see that this is an important skill, for use both in education and in being an informed citizen."

"I think you are on to something now."

REFLECT

Think of a time in your personal life when you discovered that someone who was very important to you did not value something in the same way you did. Was it about being on time to an event? Was it about including details in a report or project? If the conflict was with your spouse or partner, was it about deciding on a vacation?

Now, look at your current classroom. Do you and your learners have different views on a specific value? Do you differ about starting precisely on time? Do you differ about the amount of detail needed when assigning tasks? Is it about how you present lessons? Is it about different passions or interests regarding the topic?

In the space below, briefly describe one particular incident. Next, write why it is important to you. Then project how the learners in your classroom would view the same situation. Notice the similarities and differences. To what extent do the differences and similarities directly influence the subject being taught as opposed to the styles used in teaching and learning? What matters most?

_____

_____

_____

_____

Al Hernandez stopped by Dr. Diana Johnson's office late one afternoon, hoping to talk with her about her role with the Diversity Staff Development Committee. Diana is pleased to see Al in the office and is encouraged by his comments on how well the training is going. His real motive for being there, however, is to question his own role and behaviors on the committee. Al is wondering whether he has what it takes to deal with the varied and sometimes contentious issues around diversity.

"Dr. Johnson, you always seem to know exactly what to say in the training or with parents or teachers or community members to keep them focused on the positive side of diversity. I'm not sure I'll ever be able to do that. What else can I do to learn more about valuing diversity?"

"Al, you are being too hard on yourself. Do you think it takes a person of color to value diversity? Do you think ethnic diversity is the only difference that matters in a classroom?"

"No, not exactly, but I can't speak with the same experience and credibility that you have."

"And you're not expected to. You bring your own experiences. And your credibility is based on the high value you place on diversity, the important work that you do in opening the minds and hearts of the people you work with, affirming that differences are not deficits. That is what gives you credibility, Al. Your work demonstrates your values."

GO DEEPER

What have you learned from Al? What have you learned from the stories in this chapter? After reflecting on what you learned from this chapter, develop an activity for your colleagues to help enhance their understanding of what "valuing diversity" really means.

_____

_____

_____

_____

9 Managing the Dynamics of Difference

Culture is not a problem to be solved.

—Terry Cross[1]

Think of a classroom conflict in which you are currently embroiled or that you resolved recently. How well do you think you are handling it—or handled it? What resources do or did you have for managing it? What do you think is or was the source of the conflict?

_____

_____

_____

_____

- Assessing Culture
- Valuing Diversity
- Managing the Dynamics of Difference
- Adapting to Diversity
- Institutionalizing Cultural Knowledge

---

[1]In correspondence to authors.

School Site Council

Al had met a young couple at one of his children's sports events and decided to add them to his interview list. Alicia and Alberto are both in their early 40s and enjoy being the parents of three school-age children. Alberto is the assistant manager at MedSupplies.com. Alicia and Alberto are happy to participate in school activities with their children. Alicia was elected to serve on the School Site Council for Maple View Middle School. She also volunteered to serve as one of the parent chaperons for her son Bert's sixth-grade overnight camping trip to the local mountains. Alberto and the younger two children, Allie and Cee-Cee, joined them, so it became a family outing as well. Alberto's company, MedSupplies.com, donated the use of one of their delivery vans for the overnight school trip. Alberto stocked the van with food supplies and science equipment for the trip.

Alicia became aware of the outdoor science education program at her first School Site Council meeting for the year. When the principal said that not all students attended outdoor education, Alicia wanted to know, "Who doesn't, and why not?" One of the teachers said, "The farm kids don't go because their parents don't really care whether they go or not. They just keep them at home to add extra workers in the fields while the other kids are studying hard at outdoor education. There's nothing we can do about it if the parents don't care, is there?"

In years past, students who could not afford the trip were assigned to the library for the three days the other sixth graders were on the science trip. The students left behind were assigned written projects about outdoor science. Most of the students who could not afford the trip lived in the farmers' housing project. The families were embarrassed to send the children to school because everyone would know why they were in the library for three days. So the parents kept the children home and had them work in the fields those days to learn about the importance of rain for the crops, soil nutrients, and plants and animals living together. The children learned that good crops produced good incomes. When the children returned to school after their three days of absence, they were given grades of *F* for unexcused absences. No one at the school even questioned why so many of the farm kids were absent at the same time.

Last year, Alberto and Alicia chaired the fundraising activities for the school so that students who couldn't afford the $150 for the trip could receive scholarships to cover their costs. This year, because of Alberto and Alicia's hard work and commitment, all the children in the sixth grade took the outdoor science trip. Some teachers resent the fact that *those* kids were getting a free ride and have spoken out about the "handouts" to some kids whose parents won't even come to parent conferences. Alicia tells Al that she is perplexed that a good deed has caused some conflict at the school. She also tells Al that she has encountered similar conflicts in her workplace. "Maybe it's a Maple View thing," she says.

Conflict is a basic, natural aspect of life. For a moment, think of conflict as tension. To walk, you must coordinate the tensing and relaxing muscles in your body—including the beating of your heart muscles. Tension and conflict are vital to life, as well as to almost every other process in our universe.

Imagine a world in which everyone was exactly like you and liked everything that you liked. After a week or two, most of us would long for company that would challenge, test, entertain, or complement us. Conflict makes the world work. Without tension and the conflict that accompanies it, we would lose the benefits of creative brainstorming, group problem solving, and collective decision making. So why then do so many of us think that conflict is bad? Why do we often view conflict as a negative? Perhaps because so few of us have the necessary skills to manage conflict well.

MISMANAGING CONFLICT

It is the mismanagement of conflict, not the conflict itself, that causes most problems. In dominant American society, we are socialized to perceive conflict as something to avoid. Most of us have problems because we haven't learned to manage the conflict that precipitated the problem. Instead, we learn to ignore the conflict and maintain superficial niceties, to be polite instead of honest, to sweep conflict under the rug and dance around the huge heap of elephant dung in the middle of the room. When those tactics no longer work, we become aggressors or adversaries and we seek someone or something to blame for our dilemmas. Once you understand that conflict is normal and natural, you will not like it any more than you do now, but you will then be ready to seek ways to understand it and to manage it more effectively.

In a classroom, conflict abounds. When you relate to people in a classroom setting, you start out with a power conflict. The instructor usually has more power than the learners do. As the instructor, you control what is taught, how it is taught, and what the learners must do to receive your teaching. You choose among presentation techniques (e.g., lecture, reading, small groups, use of media, experiential activities, or project-based learning). You determine where people sit, when they can take breaks, and how their learning will be assessed. As the instructor, you may not feel as powerful as you are perceived to be, and that is another source of conflict.

You seek to have a sense of control over your classroom environment. Often, however, your supervisor seeks some control over your classroom and your instruction. Whether you work in an elementary school or are the lead trainer in a bank, someone is probably trying to have control over or input into what you teach, the materials you teach with, and in many cases how you teach.

Often, people who seek to stay in control do not have the skills to manage the conflicts that arise between them and other people who also seek to control their environments. When people have greater institutional power, they often make rules to ensure that they get their way or that the symptoms of the resulting conflict do not affect them. This is very common in the classroom. When instructors do not have the skill to manage conflict effectively, they often make rules to substitute for their lack of communication and conflict resolution skills. For example:

> Stuart Montgomery, ninth-grade teacher, is angry because two students took advantage of their hall pass privileges. "OK, we've been having this problem for too long, so from now on, no one will be allowed to use the hall pass during class. So people, take care of your business before class or after class. Once you walk through that door, you are mine until the bell rings. The only excuse for missing class is illness, and even if you get ill during class, you will still wait until the class is over to leave."

You may perceive this high school example as a bit extreme, but you might also laugh because it is very familiar. Some instructors make rules about where people sit, forcing them to move to the front and center of the room—for the instructors' comfort. Some instructors pass out papers one sheet at a time so that their learners will not read ahead. They insist that they take notes—or not take notes. They insist that their students' posture signals rapt attention—so that they are assured that their messages are getting across. They do this despite our years of study about the differences in how people think and listen and process information. Moreover, these instructional behaviors are expressed in classrooms that are relatively homogeneous. What happens when the instructor chooses to acknowledge the differences in the classroom? What happens when you invite a diversity of perspectives into the classroom?

Once you have embraced a value for diversity, conflict management poses even more challenges (Banks, 1999; McAllister & Jordan Irvine, 2000; Riehl, 2000). By acknowledging diversity as a natural process of coming together, you now recognize more people, with more differences, and you consequently have more issues over which to disagree. When you and I sit down to the table for a conversation (whomever you and I may be), we both have to remember that not only do we bring ourselves to the table, but we bring our personal histories as well. Our personal histories lead to conscious or unconscious awareness. For example, I may have issues with people who are X and you may feel uncomfortable around people who do Y.

Everyone brings their biases and prejudices, which provide the lenses through which we see and interpret everything. Also present at the table are the ghosts of our past experiences dealing with this particular issue and of our past experiences dealing with people like the person whom we face. We also bring to the table the ghosts of our parents, our families, and our friends who influence, however subtly, the way we give, receive, and interpret information. Knowing and acknowledging these realities about ourselves enables us to become culturally proficient.

Because you value diversity, you assess the variety of differences present in your classroom, assess the potential for conflict, and work to acquire skills to manage it. You may be familiar with the term *conflict resolution*. This term implies that conflict can be ended. Sometimes that is true. Most of the time, however, conflict can only be managed. That is, you cannot make the issue causing the conflict to go away, but you can help people to develop healthy responses to it. For these reasons, we prefer the term *conflict management*.

REFLECT

Think about the conflict you described in the "Get Centered" activity for this chapter. Was it your conflict with a learner or group of learners? Was it between groups of learners? Do you believe that, perhaps, the issue was more serious than it appeared at first? Describe the behaviors and feelings that you observed. Don't analyze them; just describe them.

_____

_____

_____

_____

As you read the next section, keep this situation in mind. You will be invited to take a closer look at it later in this chapter.

SOURCES OF CONFLICT

To manage conflict effectively, first determine the nature of the conflict. There are six basic categories over which people have conflicts: facts, values, perceptions, methods, personalities, and cultures (Schein, 1989). *Facts* are indisputable truths. If you are in conflict over what you think are facts, get the real facts. Collect the facts, correct what you thought were facts, and sort them from values and perceptions.

Values are strongly held beliefs that do not require facts to support them; our values are filters through which we observe what goes on in our environment. If values are the source of the conflict, it is important to clarify them and understand that it is almost impossible to change another person's values. Seek to understand different values, but don't waste time attempting to change them. People do not often change their values because someone has presented them with a persuasive argument. We change our values because of significant emotional events, such as birth, death, marriage, divorce, or life crises. Our values also change over time when we interact with someone or something that conflicts with our values and causes us to rethink a previously nonnegotiable belief.

Perceptions are our interpretations of the facts that our senses show us. Often, people mistake their perceptions for facts. If differences in perception are the cause of the conflict, check your perceptions and those of others, and share them. Invite the other parties to sit where you are so that they can see the object of conflict from your perspective. At the same time, move to where the other parties are so that you can view the object from their perspective. Clarify each observer's perceptions so that you can understand why each of you has taken your respective positions.

Ury (1991) calls this perspective taking "going to the balcony." In the theater, if you have a seventh-row center seat, you are in the best position to appreciate the sets and the makeup and the lighting. You can willfully suspend your disbelief because your perspective is perfect to appreciate the magic of the theater. If, however, you are in the balcony, your perspective changes dramatically. You may suspend your disbelief, but you also may be distracted by what else you can see. From the balcony, you have a glimpse around the sets, and you can see what is behind them. You may see the many workers who help to make the magic. You can see the lights and the pulleys that move the sets; you can see the orchestra in the pit. Because of your perspective, your understanding and appreciation of what is happening on the stage are very different than they were in your seventh-row center seat. When you go to the balcony in the midst of a conflict, you are stepping off the center stage of the drama so that you can see a bit more. Often, with greater understanding comes greater appreciation. It is then much easier to separate perceptions from facts.

Suppose that your administrator assigned forty-five students to your classroom. You may perceive that your administrator did so to punish you with extra students. Your philosophy of teaching, which is informed by your values, tells you that this overcrowding is wrong: Learners cannot thrive in an environment in which you are forced to lecture because you believe there is no space or time to teach in any other way. If you are concerned about the great number of students in your classroom, ask your administrator, "I'm confused about why I now have forty-five people in my class, when we agreed that twenty-five was the optimal number. I need help understanding what's going on?" You may learn that you are not, in fact, being punished, but that this was a way to resolve some other problem that your administrator had. You, on the other hand, reply that had your supervisor inquired, you could have provided a number of alternative solutions. You and he are now in a conflict of methodology.

Conflict in *methods* often results in an argument over whose methods will be used. Here, you need to negotiate. Is the objective to do things according to a particular process or to get a specific product? Get agreement on what is important: the process or the product. If it is the product, be sure you have established criteria for evaluating the end product, and let the people involved in the process decide which method they will use for getting that product. Again, how the conflict is managed may be influenced by who has the most institutional power or how each person in the situation perceives the power of the other. It gets complicated, but it is a negotiation that takes place daily for most people.

If you find that you are in conflict because of different *personality* styles, it is important to understand the motivating factors behind the personality. Is the person gentle or forceful, oriented toward people or toward products? Have you noticed whether your language tends to be concrete or abstract? Do you process ideas randomly or sequentially? There are many assessment tools that can help you to determine what your social style is. Your goal here is to adjust your approach to complement the other person's style of interacting so that you can better focus on the issues that concern you both.

Differences in *culture* cover a wide range of values and behaviors. Conflicts in values, perceptions, or methods may emerge because of differences in age, gender, geography, social class, or ability. Just as you will not change anyone's values, you will not change anyone's culture. To get through the conflicts arising from these differences, you must first notice that the differences among people do make a difference. Then, in collaboration with the other person, seek to understand what differences are causing conflict and then decide what would be best for the current situation. Strive to increase your own and the other person's understanding and, consequently, willingness to work toward mutually acceptable goals. This approach works reasonably well when the conflict is between two people with a sophisticated collection of conflict management tools.

With a larger and presumably more diverse group, you will need a wider range of conflict management skills. If you have good conflict management skills now, congratulations. We invite you to develop a still higher level of skills so that you can manage the subtle nuances of cultural differences. The principle of intentionality, proceeding with the conscious intention of doing something differently, applies here. The more intention and attention you give to the process, the more positive will be the outcomes you achieve. If your intention is to notice the different ways that people respond to your questions, you will learn, over time, to recognize or inquire when you suspect that the men and women give gender-specific responses to certain types of questions.

Human Resources Team

The Leadership Maple View committee has been meeting to determine the scope of its new project. Committee members have expressed their own views and ideas about the current leadership theme, "Growing Our Own Leaders." Dr. Montanaro Director of Human Resources served as moderator for the opening sessions. Dr. Montanaro begins the third meeting of the group by saying: "The purpose of tonight's meeting is to reach consensus about the leadership project for this year. We have heard several suggestions in our previous meetings, all of which are consistent with the charge at our first meeting. We have been asked by our board and superintendent to develop a community-based service project. Let's continue to brainstorm other ideas; then we can clarify these ideas and narrow the list to determine our top priorities and, finally, choose the project on which we will focus our energy and resources for the year."

Carol Cheng says, "I like how you have outlined our work here tonight. Many of us have busy work schedules, and having this clear purpose will help us get right down to our new project."

"Yeah, me too," Stu Montgomery says. "Those of us who are teachers hardly have time to do any of the extra community stuff as it is. So, let's talk about who wants to do what. I think we need to do something to help the poor families over on the East Side catch up with their schoolwork. We could probably set up some community sports clubs, too, to help out some of the families over there."

"Excuse me, Mr. Montgomery," Alberto Alvarez interrupts, "but you make it sound like 'over there' is not even part of Maple View. As a matter of fact, the East Side was the only side until a few years ago. People like my father helped build this community, and he would want us to work together on this leadership project. You make it sound like the poor people on the East Side need some special attention."

"Now wait a minute," Stu protests. "That's not what I said at all. Your people are highly respected in this town. You have worked hard for everything you have. It's just that some people don't really care about what their kids do after school or in the neighborhood. Some parents don't care how their kids do in school. We have to help those kids."

"Mr. Montgomery," Alicia Alvarez says, "I wish more teachers would take the time to learn about what parents really think and care about, before they assume that parents don't care. I know that some parents care greatly for their children and they trust the lives of their children to the teachers and schools of this community. Do you think the parents on the West Side care more about their children than the parents on the East Side of town?"

"Hey, now wait a minute." Stu protests, "This isn't fair. . . . I'm not a racist. . . ."

Dr. Montanaro steps in. "OK, hold on Stu. No one called you a racist. Members of the committee have brought up some interesting questions. Maybe it's time that we dealt with what some folks in this city call the 'East Side story.' Stu, I heard your defensive comments, and I believe that they come from your sincere desire to serve the children of this city. These are emotional issues that the committee must be willing to deal with. Our community deals with them daily. My hope is that we are willing to present our views and ideas in an open and honest forum. We will not all agree, but perhaps we can start by examining what keeps us from hearing viewpoints that differ from our own. Now, I'll chart some of the issues that I've heard here tonight so that we can continue to keep them in front of us."

Let's review the six conflict management strategies:

1. Get the facts.

2. Clarify values.

3. Check perceptions.

4. Negotiate methods.

5. Adjust to personalities.

6. Seek to understand cultural differences.

Figure 9.1 invites you to look at these conflict management strategies from both the individual and the organizational perspectives.

Figure 9.1 Management Strategies for Various Sources of Conflict

Sources of Conflict	Management Strategy	For Individuals		For Organizations	
		Within the Person	Between Persons	Within the Organization	Between Organizations
Facts	Determine what the facts actually are.		X	X	X
Values	Distinguish your core values from your strong opinions. Communicate your values clearly, remembering that people don't easily change their values and that sometimes you may have to engage in activities that conflict with your personal values.	X	X	X	X
Perceptions	Separate your perceptions from the facts. Ask questions to learn how the other person perceives the situation.	X	X	X	X
Methods	Ask yourself, is your way important, or is it just important that you have your way?	X	X	X	X
Personalities	Recall your understanding of social styles to make the appropriate adjustments.		X		
Cultures	Engage in a learning conversation to discern why you want to do something or engage with someone in a particular way. Decide with the other party what would best serve everyone's needs in the particular situation.		X	X	X

REFLECT

Review the conflict situation you identified in this chapter's "Getting Centered" activity. Can you describe the source of the conflict in each of your own examples? Look at Figure 9.1, and with a colleague decide if you used an appropriate strategy for addressing the conflict.

_____

_____

_____

_____

STRATEGIES FOR MANAGING CONFLICT

The preceding section described the sources of conflict. We now invite you to focus on the various ways that people manage conflict. Figure 9.2 illustrates the five different strategies discussed in this section.

To manage conflict requires courage, trust, and commitment; it also requires you to apply the principle of intentionality. You cannot wish conflict away or simply hope that you will manage it. Instead, you must attend closely to the people and the situation, and you must begin with the intention of managing the tension. You must think about what you want and then anticipate how you might act differently to manage the tension in that particular situation.

As an instructor, not only do you have situations in which you are in conflict with someone—your colleague, your supervisor, or one of the learners in your classroom—but you also are called on to mediate conflicts between people in your classroom. Each of us has a preferred style for managing conflict. Those of us who handle conflict effectively use a style that is appropriate for the situation. The five most common styles of conflict management are avoidance, accommodation, compromise, competition, and collaboration.

When _avoiding_ conflict, people do not immediately pursue their own concerns or those of the other person. They simply do not address the conflict. This avoidance may take the form of diplomatically sidestepping an issue, postponing an issue until a better time, or simply withdrawing from a threatening situation. You are avoiding conflict if you don't deal with the troublesome issue, and you continue to let the conflict simmer in the background. Avoiding often becomes a lose-lose situation because neither of you gets what you want, and both of you may end up losing the relationship. Avoidance is effective when you are not vested in the relationship and

Figure 9.2 Approaches to Managing Conflict

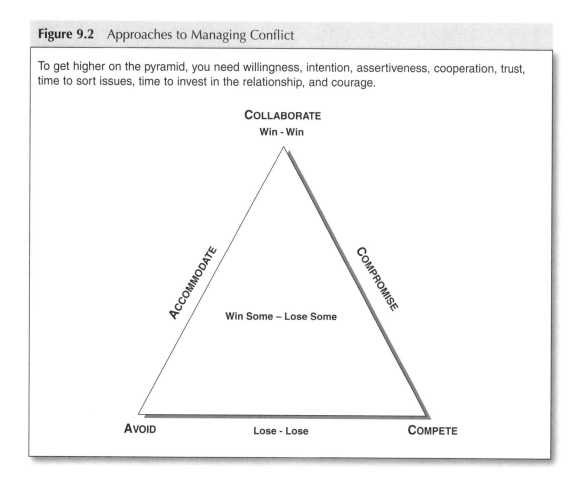

To get higher on the pyramid, you need willingness, intention, assertiveness, cooperation, trust, time to sort issues, time to invest in the relationship, and courage.

COLLABORATE
Win - Win

ACCOMMODATE

COMPROMISE

Win Some – Lose Some

AVOID   Lose - Lose   COMPETE

you don't care about the issue. If you have a learner who constantly baits you or others in the room, you may avoid the conflict by not recognizing that learner. On the other hand, if two learners are constantly bickering, avoiding a confrontation with them will only lead to further classroom disruptions.

When *accommodating,* people subsume their own concerns to satisfy the concerns of the other person; there is an element of self-sacrifice in this style. Accommodation may take the form of selfless generosity or charity, obeying another person's unpleasant or undesirable order, or yielding to another's point of view. You are accommodating when you go along with the other person because you don't want to make waves. This is a win some–lose some situation. You lose the issue to the other person; the other person loses the benefit of your ideas and perceptions, and you both win a little peace and the perception of harmony. If you are trying to teach a new concept by using a technique that is effective but that the learners don't particularly like, you may win congeniality points by giving in, but you also lose teaching time, and the learners may lose an important learning experience.

When *compromising,* people seek to find some expedient, mutually acceptable solution that partially satisfies both parties. It falls on a middle ground between competing and accommodating. Compromise strategies address an issue more directly than avoidance strategies do. On the other hand, compromise strategies don't explore the issue in as much depth as collaboration strategies do. Compromising might mean splitting the difference, exchanging concessions, or seeking a quick middle-ground position. You give a little to get a little. So does the other person. Compromise is also a win some–lose some situation. Each of you gets something that you want, and each of you loses something that you want. Instructors in preK–12 schools do this all the time, as they bargain with their students for compliance and cooperation. At some point in the careers of instructors who have compromise as their dominant style, they have to make tough choices between covering the breadth of material in their curriculum or taking fewer topics and covering them in depth so that the learners can use the information outside of the classroom.

When *competing,* people pursue their own concerns at the other person's expense, and they use whatever seems appropriate to win their own position. The outcome of this power-oriented management strategy may depend on a person's ability to argue, the person's position, or even threats of harm. Competing might mean standing up for your rights, defending a position that you believe is correct, or simply trying to win. You should compete when the issue is so important that you are willing to risk losing everything in order to win. This is often a lose-lose approach because even if you win, you may lose the relationship because of the tactics you used to win. The best instructors we have observed use cooperative learning strategies far more often than competitive ones. The reduced level of tension and the increased learner-to-learner interaction results in an environment that is conducive to moving toward Cultural Proficiency.

When *collaborating,* people try to work with one another to find some solution that fully satisfies the concerns of both persons. It means digging into an issue to identify the underlying concerns of the two individuals and striving to find an alternative that addresses both sets of concerns. Collaboration between two persons may take the form of exploring a disagreement to learn from each other's insights, resolving some condition that would otherwise require them to compete for resources, or confronting and trying to find a creative solution to an interpersonal problem. You should collaborate when the issue and the relationship are equally important to you. Collaboration requires that you invest the time to sort facts and perceptions, to prioritize the issues, to clarify what you really want, and then to figure out a way for you both to get what you want (Thomas & Kilmann, 1974).

Because collaboration takes a great deal of time and energy, we do not recommend that you collaborate on every issue. When the relationship is as important as the issue, the investment in collaboration pays off. Collaboration is important as instructors work with other professionals to set long-range goals, determine curriculum, and learn new instructional strategies. Similarly, collaboration is beneficial to the classroom when the instructor uses these skills to engage learners in problem-solving and discovery-learning activities. In these situations, learners will acquire effective communication and problem-solving skills while working with others to solve complex tasks or problems.

REFLECT

What is a situation in your work environment in which collaboration was used to manage a conflict? What have been some situations in your classroom when you have used collaborative teaching strategies? What benefit have you seen for the learners in these situations?

_____

_____

_____

_____

ENGAGE

Look again at your examples of conflict and decide if your approach was appropriate for the situation, for your intention, and for the attention you gave to the situation.

_____

_____

_____

_____

GO DEEPER

How do you describe your style of dealing with conflict? How is conflict handled in your classroom? How is it addressed among your colleagues? What skills do you currently possess in this area? What skills would you like to develop? What determines if the strategy you are using is a culturally proficient?

_____

_____

_____

_____

10 Adapting to Diversity

If we notice [learners] taking different paths we can interact with their different journeys just as we would alter our talking to adapt to our listeners and in a couple of years expect them to arrive at common outcomes.

—Mary M. Clay[1]

GET CENTERED

Have you ever told yourself you wanted to change without really intending to do anything differently? Think of a time you made a decision to be different. Perhaps you decided to exercise more, to go on a diet, or to stop smoking. Did these changes affect anyone other than you? Did you need anyone else's cooperation to implement the change? What steps did you take to ensure that you would change? Did you make the change you set out to make? What do you suppose is the difference between a decision and a commitment?

_____

_____

_____

_____

[1]Sennett (2004), p. 28.

- Assessing Culture
- Valuing Diversity
- Managing the Dynamics of Difference
- Adapting to Diversity
- Institutionalizing Cultural Knowledge

A New Role

Al goes across the hall to talk with a long time colleague, Dr. Alicia Adams. After receiving her PhD six years ago, Alicia asked her colleagues to call her "Dr. Adams" in front of the high school students. One teacher responded by saying, "Well, I guess you have to be a role model for the black kids, but you'll always be 'Miss 'Licia to me."

Dr. Alicia Adams is African American and in her mid-40s. She moved to Maple View as a high school English teacher. She completed her administrative training at State University during her tenth year as a teacher, after which she was quickly promoted to assistant principal at Pine Hills High School. Some members of the community and many faculty members at the high school felt that Alicia received her promotion as part of the district's affirmative action program. Alicia was aware of the perception that her colleagues had, and had decided to prove herself by being an outstanding assistant principal.

"Of course, I was excited, but I knew it wouldn't take much," Alicia mused, "to outperform the other assistant principal, Mr. Anderson." Fred Anderson had been the assistant principal at the high school for fifteen years when Alicia joined the administrative staff. In charge of student suspensions and facility supervision, Fred had shown little initiative and knew very little about helping learners and instructors be more effective in the classrooms. He functioned more as an administrative assistant than he did as an educator. The staff viewed him as "our assistant principal," serving their needs first and students' needs last.

The current principal, Dr. Robert Hanford, told Alicia during her first meeting with him, "Now, young lady, you are going to show people around here that you are just as good as they are. Just like you have done all your life, you'll have to prove to some people that you are smarter than they think you are. I want to make sure that you are successful at this job. The first thing you need to do is enroll in a doctoral program. That'll show 'em. Nobody was surprised when I got my PhD. That was expected of me. But, not you. No, they don't expect that you can do it. It's up to you to prove them wrong, so others who come after you won't have to overcome low, or no, expectations.

"Let's start by giving you Mr. Anderson's office. It's much larger and has nicer furniture in it. I'll move him to an office in the other building. He'll be fine with the move, I'm sure."

Alicia spent her first year as assistant principal trying to repair the damage done by the principal's well-intended decision to move Fred's office and give Alicia the better office space. In contrast, the best thing Bob did for Alicia was to recommend her to the State University doctoral program. Four years later, after Bob retired, she became Dr. Alicia Adams and the new principal. Fred was promoted to director of the Community School.

Alicia has been highly successful in designing professional development that includes a focus on culturally proficient classrooms and schools. She tells Al that she is aware of the different perception of the community's great divide, the story of the East Side/West Side. "No one wants to talk about it," she says, "but it has been the impetus for my choosing to focus our staff development efforts of developing cultural competence. If I have to endure unintentional and sometimes stupid slights, acts of paternalism, or sometimes just outright racism and prejudice, then what do you think happens to many of our students? I really don't think that most teachers mean to be hurtful, but I do know that there is a lot of cultural ignorance throughout the system. We are all changing. How we adapt to those changes is the key to our growth and progress."

It is very easy to decide to change. You say, "Sure," to yourself or whomever is pestering you, and you stay the same. Making a commitment to change, however, is quite different. When you make a commitment to change, you must work hard to realign your activities and your approach to life to accommodate that change.

Change is easiest when you are in total control of whatever you're changing. You probably rather like it when you decide to rearrange the furniture in your home or when you decide to be with friends instead of family for a holiday celebration. As long as you live alone and reside in a location many hours from your family, you can implement these decisions without having to consult with anyone and without any major repercussions. Moreover, besides the physical exertion of moving furniture, you can decide to change, and then implement the change with very little effort. Too bad that not all change is this easy.

A COMMITMENT TO CHANGE

The easiest thing to change is your mind. You can do that lying in bed, half-asleep, watching late-night television. It is much harder to change your behavior and to make the change last over time. It is also much more difficult to change when your change depends on the cooperation of others or when the change requires you to acquire a new set of behaviors. Anyone can stop smoking or go on a diet for the next fifteen minutes, but to consistently engage in the new behavior for the next fifteen months requires a very different type of effort and commitment.

Again, the principle of intentionality, proceeding with the conscious intention of doing something differently, applies to the commitment to change. To implement a change, you must pay attention to how you are doing things now, then make a conscious decision to do things differently. The more specific you are about how differently you will do things, the greater your likelihood of actually doing it. You also must engage in each situation that calls for the new behavior with the intention of doing so in a different way.

REFLECT

Are you engaged in a change today? Are you truly committed to that change?

_____

_____

_____

_____

_____

Your commitment to change is the key to becoming culturally proficient. Cultural Proficiency is a process; becoming culturally proficient is not a onetime event like moving your furniture around. It is more like quitting smoking or going on a diet, in that each day you have to decide again whether this is what you want to do. It is a change of lifestyle, a change in how you view the world around you.

You must become aware of the situations that invite culturally proficient behavior and then pay attention to them so that your behavior will be different—each time. Becoming culturally proficient requires you to change on a number of levels. The first level is overcoming your unawareness of the need to adapt, which we described in Chapter 5 on barriers to Cultural Proficiency. Thus, you must first recognize that your current actions are not having the effect you would like in a particular environment. Next, you move through the essential elements as you seek to relate to this environment with Cultural Proficiency.

By assessing culture—your own culture and that of your organization—you begin to understand how your instructional behaviors and the organization's practices affect people—both members of the dominant group and members of oppressed, marginalized groups. By valuing diversity, you become more aware of how your prejudices and stereotypes influence the judgments you make and the way you treat the learners you teach. Your greater awareness, coupled with your conflict management skills, helps you manage the dynamics of difference.

At this point, your environment may be a little unstable. It is time now for you to adapt to diversity. By adapting to diversity, you will make some permanent changes in your values and behaviors and in your organization's policies and practices. These changes will reflect how you and the diverse people in your environment adapt to one another.

The Pine Hills High School Professional Learning Community (PLC) is reviewing their data on student achievement using the statewide assessment data. Clair, a tenth-grade English teacher, notices that the English learners (ELs) are the demographic group with the lowest scores.

"Look, once again, our ELs are keeping us from reaching our target scores." Clair laments.

"Well, that's why they call it the *achievement gap*. Our English speakers are doing very well, as usual." Her colleague Jim responds. The PLC had been working on their action plan for improving instruction and closing the achievement gap as part of the schoolwide plan.

"The kids from the East Side will never learn to speak English as long as their parents speak Spanish at home. And, those new families moving in from who knows where, speaking who knows what . . . you know . . . how will we ever improve our test scores?" asks Jan, one of the more senior teachers at the high school.

After several minutes, Erin, the PLC leader, says, "Well, I know how frustrated we are about these test scores. And, I am wondering if the kids are at fault here. Maybe we have to ask ourselves some questions. Last week at our staff development day, Dr. Anderson asked us to use the essential elements to look at our PLC work. Remember, she asked us to examine how we were specifically 'adapting to diversity' of our community. Well, are we adapting to the needs of our ELs? What are we doing to meet their needs?"

REFLECT

Think about your school or organization. Can you remember a time in the recent past when you or your school failed to adapt to the needs of groups of students? What is an example of something you or your organization did to adapt to the needs of new members? How about in your classroom? What examples can you think of when you adapted or failed to adapt to the needs of some learners?

_____

_____

_____

_____

In the case story, the PLC made a decision to move toward Cultural Proficiency as a team and as individual teachers after several meetings and lengthy dialogue. Once you and your organization decide to become more culturally proficient, you must decide as well how serious you are. To take action requires more than a decision. The essential elements give impetus to those decisions to move forward.

Change requires a commitment from the organization, as well as from the individuals who work there. In a committed, monogamous relationship, the partners make a covenant with each other. Their vows are sacred, and implied in the promises they make to each other is the agreement that they will change to accommodate each other's presence in their lives. Clearly, a marriage commitment requires a great deal of effort if the relationship is to work.

Similarly, the commitment to achieving Cultural Proficiency in your organization requires continual hard work. You must relentlessly look deeply at your own biases, values, and behaviors. You must constantly watch for both overt and benign discrimination in organizational policies and must continually assess the cultural competency of your organization's practices.

At one of the monthly meetings of Leadership Maple View, current members are listening to Nikos Papadopoulos, their diversity consultant, talk to them about Cultural Proficiency. Nikos is encouraging them to move beyond planning cultural events and special activities around ethnic-specific holidays. The group is flummoxed. For years, the chamber of commerce has sponsored an ethnic food fair in the downtown area. This year, Leadership Maple View plans to cosponsor the event. They already have plans to bring in mariachi bands, African drummers, a bagpipe orchestra, and the New Metropolis Tongan Dancers. They are so proud of all their plans to celebrate the diversity of Maple View.

"What are we supposed to do now," Leonard Williams groans, "cancel our plans?"

"No," replies Nikos. "Don't cancel your plans. Just realize that once you have knowledge, nothing is going to look the same to you. As you move toward Cultural Proficiency, you will continue to assess and rethink activities that you have taken for granted in the past. What I was trying to do is invite you to focus more on yourselves. Who are you as a cultural entity? How does who you are affect the people around you? What are the various cultures represented in your classrooms and training rooms? How do they interplay and interact with one another?"

"Wait a minute," Julie says. "What does culture have to do with teaching math or English literature?"

"At the hospital we have similar issues of Cultural Proficiency. How can we ask nurses to learn about all the cultures that pass through this hospital?" Alicia pipes in. "And you know that we can never make doctors do anything. They already think they know everything. We want to do better, but with this Cultural Proficiency, you are asking us to change the way we do everything!"

REFLECT

What questions would you ask the consultant? If you were the consultant, how would you respond? In your school or organization, what is done now to overtly address the issues arising from diversity? In your view, what else needs to be done as a first step?

_____

_____

_____

_____

When an organization makes a commitment to Cultural Proficiency, everybody must change. This requirement explains why most organizations do not move far beyond special events that celebrate ethnic diversity. As you move toward Cultural Proficiency, go deeper as organizations and as individuals. Explore and acknowledge the subtler, yet more profound aspects of culture. Look beyond physical type and language to see the difference that differences make on an everyday basis. As with any other committed relationship, you and the other participants in your organization engage in a constant give and take, as each of you adjusts to the other. As a culturally proficient instructor, you must facilitate major and minor adjustments in the culture of your school or organization and in your classroom as well.

Adaptations to diversity are sometimes easier to see at the level of organizational policy and practices, and they may be more difficult to observe in your own classroom behavior. Take a moment now to examine the values that inform how you do the following.

- Select materials for instruction.
- Decide on your techniques for presenting materials.
- Watch for how learners subtly respond to your choices.
- Facilitate healthy conversations among the learners.
- Mediate conflicts among learners.
- Take advantage of teachable moments, as reflected in the following example.

For the first two days of a ten-day professional development class, one of the learners sat in the back of the room, and whenever she spoke, she used a throaty, scratchy, soft voice. After a few such whispery comments, the instructor became annoyed with the woman. "Please, speak so people can hear you," the instructor implored. "Speak up please," the instructor reminded her each time. At the beginning of the second day, the woman approached the instructor and said, "You keep insisting that I speak up for everyone to hear. I just wanted you to know that not all handicaps are visible. I have damaged vocal chords and cannot speak above my stage whisper."

REFLECT

What do you see as the adaptation issues in this teachable moment? How would you respond to each example?

_____

_____

_____

_____

In Chapter 9 on managing the dynamics of difference, we discussed the dynamics of power in the classroom. As an instructor, you have the power that comes from your role, and most of the learners accede to that power. As we're sure you know, the learners have a lot of power as well. They have the power of noncooperation, the power to disrupt, the power of noncompliance, the power to withdraw or not participate, and the power to not show up.

In elementary classrooms, learners often play an overt game of bullying and one-upmanship with their fellow classmates. In a classroom of adults, the games are still played, but the tactics are subtler and the consequences more profound. Some instructors encounter learners who bring out the worst in them. They respond by bullying, speaking over them, interrupting them, ignoring them, picking on them, and refusing to acknowledge them when they seek to contribute in the classroom. As a culturally proficient instructor, you will recognize when you are overusing your power or using it inappropriately, and you will change what you do to adapt to the diversity in your classroom.

Culturally proficient instructors look for opportunities to adapt to diversity by asking: Who else might want to speak? Let's hear another point of view. What might be another way to approach this issue? Who is not here that we need to hear from? What haven't we thought of yet? Who might help us see a different point of view? These questions are designed to help learners explore new ideas and adapt to new ways of thinking.

REFLECT

In your classroom, who is the oppressor and who are the oppressed? If you say no one, spend a few days observing yourself and your learners. Who has the power and how is it used? Who is scapegoated, teased, ignored, interrupted, ridiculed, punished, or penalized? Do you notice any patterns? How does the scapegoat's behavior differ from that of the other learners in the classroom? Are the scapegoats really doing anything wrong? Who does the scapegoating, teasing, ignoring, interrupting, ridiculing, punishing, and penalizing? What must change?

_____

_____

_____

_____

LEARNING ORGANIZATIONS

Imagine working in a place that never learned from its mistakes and was always reinventing the proverbial wheel. This nightmarish dystopia keeps no historical records of what was done in the past and how it worked. The people from each department do not talk with people from other departments, so no one really knows what is going on at an organizational level. Consequently, resources are not shared; information is held closely until it does no one any good. There is no cross-training, and orientation rarely helps newly hired personnel to adjust to the organization's culture. This organization does not learn and is therefore not a "learning organization" (Senge, Kleiner, Roberts, Ross, & Smith, 1994; Senge et al., 1999; Wheatley, 1994).

A learning organization takes advantage of its successes and failures by talking about them and learning from them. No new project is begun without first seeing what can be learned and used from past activities. In this type of organization, the walls between the departments are porous: People are encouraged to talk with one another, sharing information and resources. People dissect their successes with as much curiosity as they do their failures. If you succeed only by accident, you minimize your chances of repeating your success. Here again, we see the principle of intentionality. Pay attention to what you are doing and go into each activity with the intention of being better—of being culturally proficient. After completing an activity, take the time to debrief, so that you and all who are involved can learn from the experience (Wheatley & Kellner-Rogers, 1995).

GUIDELINES FOR A LEARNING CONVERSATION

At the classroom level, you can apply the idea of being a learning organization by engaging the learners in learning conversations. With your colleagues, you can build a professional learning community by using guidelines that will help you to engage in conversations that are marked by candor and compassion. Courageous conversations are balanced by a desire to discover more about oneself and a commitment to be gentle as you share your truths and perceptions. Before bludgeoning someone with a hurtful fact just because it is true, ask yourself:

- Is it true?
- Is it necessary?
- Is it kind?

If it is true and necessary, consider how you might present your observation so that the conversation is kept open and the listener doesn't shut down or attack you in defense.

The guidelines for a courageous learning conversation are few and simple.

- Slow down.
- Listen first, to understand.
- Suspend certainty.
- Encourage differences.
- Make your requests clearly.
- Speak from your own experience. Use *I* statements

1. *Slow down.* Take all the time you need to give your full attention to the task. If the task is to debrief a learning experience or to mediate a conflict, set aside the time to do it. Don't rush through your professional development sessions, savor the opportunity to converse at length and deeply with your colleagues.

2. *Listen to understand.* Many listen to hear when the speaker breathes so that they can jump in, or they listen to hear how wrong the speaker is going to be. Others just look as though they are listening, when they are really just waiting to make their points. If you listen to understand, you are assuming, as Virginia Satir (1972) said, that something about what the speaker is saying is right. You are listening to hear what that is.

3. *Suspend certainty.* Suspend the certainty that you are right. Suspend the certainty that you know everything you need to know. Suspend the certainty that the speaker is wrong—again. When you suspend certainty, your walls are less rigid and your boundaries are more flexible. You are ready to learn.

4. *Encourage differences.* Listen to opinions and perspectives that differ from yours. Encourage your learners and your colleagues to challenge you to learn and grow from those differences.

5. *Speak from your own experience.* You have as much voice as you use. Use *I* statements. What you say will be much more powerful if you say *I* and speak

about your own experience, instead of using the vague and generic *you* or the nonspecific *them.* Talk about what you have observed or experienced. Avoid projecting your assumptions onto your perceptions of others.

Debriefing Questions

Guidelines for a learning conversation will help you get started and stay focused. When you are ending the conversation, it is important to take the time to assess what you did and how well you did it. The following debriefing questions may help you in that process.

- What did you notice?
- What surprised you?
- What was missing for you?
- What did you get?
- How can you use it?
- What do we as a group want to do or change?

1. *What did you notice?* The learners may not be prepared to talk about what they noticed, so you may need to repeat the question gently. What did you notice? What did you notice about yourself? What did you notice about the people in your group? What did you notice about the process? What did you notice? This question is particularly useful when you are working with people who are quick to state what was wrong and what ought to be done next. This question asks people to slow down, and it invites people to notice the subtler aspects of the situation, including the nonverbal behavior. Answers to this question often result in greater insights and learning.

2. *What surprised you?* This question (as opposed to "What did you dislike?") invites people to speak nonjudgmentally about whatever happened.

3. *What was missing for you?* This question asks people to describe what they were looking for and didn't get. It invites the learners to speak for themselves and not for anyone else. This question is particularly helpful when people in the group tend to generalize their experiences to the entire population. "What was missing for you?" refocuses them on their own experiences.

4. *What did you get?* Sometimes when the instructor asks, "What did you learn?" the learners reply, "Nothing!" This question is a bit broader and invites the learners to think broadly about their experience.

5. *How can you use it?* This question helps the learner make the transfer from the learning experience to an application in life outside the classroom.

6. *What do we as a group want to do or change?* This question implies that each individual's actions have implications for the entire group.

Here are some phrases that may help to break down conversation barriers.

- I need to think about that.
- That has not been my experience.
- What is our goal here?
- Help me understand . . .
- What are our options?
- Is there another way we can do this?
- Will you talk more about . . .?
- What will this mean for . . .?
- What I heard you say is . . .
- How does this support our goal?
- What are your concerns?
- Tell me more about . . .
- I can't listen that fast; would you talk a little slower?
- I'm not sure if I said that clearly. What did you understand me to say?
- What are some experiences that shape your perspective?
- What might be another way we can think about this issue?
- Who else needs to be at the table?
- In what ways does this decision support our learners?

ENGAGE

Try using these debriefing questions the next time you lead an activity. Notice the difference in the quality of responses and in the tone of the room by asking the softer questions that invite the learners to go deeper in their exploration of what they have learned. You may record what you notice here.

_____

_____

_____

_____

INCLUSIVE LANGUAGE AND MATERIALS

You may find many more new ways of engaging in the classroom as you move toward Cultural Proficiency. Talk with your colleagues about classroom practices that involve more people, that acknowledge invisible handicaps, and that use inclusive language. *Inclusive language* is the use of words and phrases that embrace each member of the group. No one is treated or viewed as an outsider, and no one feels like an outsider. This may mean learning to say a few phrases in the native language of your learners. Beware not to make the same mistake that the professor at the State University did in Chapter 6, when he spoke bad Spanish to Portuguese students. Talk with your learners about their learning styles and encourage them to critically reflect on their texts.

Now some instructors will say, "We have no choice about textbooks. We have to teach what the district tells us. Besides, there is no culture in math." We answer by noting, "Everything is culture bound." When stuck with inadequate textbooks, you can teach your learners to examine their texts to see whose story is being told. You also can encourage them to seek supplemental materials that add to what is in the text when giving them assignments. As for math not being culture bound, include anecdotal comments about how Greeks, Romans, Arabs, Chinese, and Egyptians contributed to various mathematical processes and theories. Such comments may be just the spark a learner needs to engage with the material. Just think of the high-level thinking skills employed in such activities—analysis and synthesis that are basic to problem solving.

A very bright student we know struggled through her first year of Hebrew and passed only with the help of a generous tutor and take-home exams. Some time after that, when exploring the Kabbala, she learned that each Hebrew letter had a mystical significance. Her comment was, "If I had only known about this aspect of the language when I was studying, it would have been a lot more interesting and would have made it a lot easier for me." We thought that it would have been a lot more work, but because her interest was piqued, she would have done the extra work enthusiastically.

Learning what you can do to enhance the cultural knowledge in your classroom may take extra work on your part. We hope that your interest will be piqued as well. Just as a committed relationship requires the work of both partners, Cultural Proficiency requires the commitment and work of those who aspire to it. You may need to take or give special classes or workshops initially to build your skills in assessing curriculum and in acquiring the knowledge to supplement them. You also may need to set aside special times for engaging in learning conversations with your colleagues about your *praxis*, the practice of your teaching craft.

ENGAGE

With your colleagues, reflect on the following questions: What are you doing? What are the values that inform your choices? How are people responding to your work? How are you growing and changing because of your intention to become a culturally proficient instructor?

COMMUNITIES OF PRACTICE

An outgrowth of and corollary to your involvement in learning conversations with your colleagues and in your classrooms is that you also will be building your own community of practice. We belong to many communities of practice (Wenger, 1998). A *community of practice* is any group to which you belong that has specific knowledge unique to that group, a particular way of doing things, and members who are identified by behaviors reflecting this knowledge and way of doing things.

Your communities of practice may include your family, your work group, your sorority, or your church congregation. Geographical lines do not mark communities in this sense. A community of practice is a psychosocial community, bound by its group identity and its group practice. As an instructor, your place of employment may be an unintentional community of practice that you would not have chosen for yourself. You may be part of an organization that has policies and practices clustering around the points of cultural incapacity and cultural blindness on the Cultural Proficiency continuum. In this case, this community of practice would be decidedly unintentional for you.

In addition to various unintentional communities of practice, you may be part of at least one *intentional community of practice,* one that you have chosen for yourself that includes a group of instructors who have made a commitment to examine their praxis. This community becomes your intentional community of practice—a community of learners. The key to intentional communities of practice is the extent to which people discuss, formally or informally, their praxis.

The other intentional community of practice to which you belong is your classroom. As you teach, you convey your values in overt and covert ways. The learners in your classroom will respond to one another within the boundaries you set and in accord with the examples of your own behavior. The classroom therefore becomes a community of practice in which you offer a silent or direct invitation to grow toward Cultural Proficiency along with you. In this way, you are creating a community of learners within your community of practice. Etienne Wenger (1998) admonishes us that in a community of practice, we understand that learning is a process of participation, whether for those who are new to the group or for those who have been there a long time. Culturally proficient learners understand that learning is continuous and ongoing. It is not limited to a particular classroom or to certain hours during the day.

Culturally proficient instructors place the emphasis on learning rather than on teaching by finding ways to use and develop the teachable moments that occur in the daily activities of the learners. In culturally proficient classrooms, both the instructors and the learners are engaged in designing activities that will enhance and enrich their learning experiences and their interactions with one another. Within this community of practice, the instructor will explore with the learners the interrelationship between what is going on in the classroom and what the learners do outside the classroom as they engage with other communities of practice (Wenger, 1998).

GO DEEPER

Identify some of your own communities of practice. Are you currently in a psychosocial community in which you can explore your culturally proficient praxis?

_____

_____

_____

_____

Observe yourself for a few weeks and notice how (or whether) you invite the learners in your classroom to engage in culturally proficient behavior. What aspects of your community of practice are you considering changing after reading this chapter?

_____

_____

_____

_____

11 Institutionalizing Cultural Knowledge

Charismatic leaders often do more harm than good because, at best, they provide episodic involvement followed by frustrated or despondent dependency. Superhuman leaders also do us another disservice: they are role models who can never be emulated by large numbers. Deep and sustained reform depends on many of us, not just on the very few who are destined to be extraordinary.

—Michael Fullan[1]

GET CENTERED

Think about when you first started the job you have now. Remember how you felt and how you reacted as you learned the norms and expectations of your employer, colleagues, and clients. Think about what you know now and how you learned it. What kinds of experiences and information would you include if you designed the orientation for yourself?

_____

_____

_____

_____

---

[1]Sennett (2004), p. 28.

- Assessing Culture
- Valuing Diversity
- Managing the Dynamics of Difference
- Adapting to Diversity
- Institutionalizing Cultural Knowledge

The East Side/West Story

Al Hernandez enters Superintendent Sandra Patton's office. Dr. Patton has been an innovative leader since her arrival in Maple View. Al and Sandra have developed a close personal and professional relationship. Al knows that Sandra plans to retire in two years and the two of them have discussed what traits they would like to see in the next superintendent. The topic then turns to Al's recent concerns. Al asks Sandra, "What do you think that we can do to address the real East Side/West Side division that still seems to exist in this community?"

Sandra says, "It's a systemic issue. It's embedded in the very fabric of the community and it must be unraveled one thread at a time. What I mean, Alberto, is that we will have to exert leadership and use all of the influence to engage the powerbrokers downtown to join us in addressing some of the social injustices across the community. At the same time we will continue to engage all faculty and members of the staff in learning community discussions and activities that make us explore our policies, practices, and procedures to ensure that they are culturally sensitive and appropriate. It is my goal to leave processes in place so that dealing with the issues of diversity is ongoing and a natural part of the growth for all Maple View personnel." Al nods in agreement as Sandra continues. "It won't be easy, but it's the legacy that I intend to leave. If we can accomplish it, this district will become the envy of many and a beacon of hope for others who dare to take big risks."

People who are culturally proficient want to learn about new cultures. They want to learn how to navigate in new cultures. They solicit feedback from members of new cultures in order to improve their effectiveness in communicating and solving problems. Likewise, culturally proficient schools and other organizations highly value learning about the cultures that are present within them. Culturally proficient instructors want to learn about the various cultures represented in their classroom. They recognize that in learning about other cultures, they will continuously expand their knowledge. These instructors also know that learning about other cultures is basic to being effective instructors. As effective instructors, they directly help some learners and indirectly serve as a role model to all learners.

LEARNING ABOUT CULTURES

The essential element *institutionalizing cultural knowledge* is comprised of learning and teaching about other cultures, including the culture of your own organization, and learning and teaching about how other people experience those cultures. Learning about other cultures goes much deeper than the typical *heroes, holidays, and haute cuisine* or *food, fun,* and *fiesta* activities in which many organizations typically engage. Clearly, these activities may serve as an entry point for some learners or as part of a greater menu of experiences that promise ever-deeper learning. In addition to these activities, however, culturally proficient instructors want to know the history, the accomplishments, and the trials and tribulations of the people of a given culture.

For culturally proficient instructors, a culturally diverse classroom is a learning laboratory. Through meeting people from other cultures, these instructors are motivated to read, to have conversations, and to reflect on their own responses to others. Their curiosity knows no bounds. They understand that teaching learners from their own culture differs from teaching learners from cultures other than theirs. At the same time, they understand that the differences that make a difference center on worldview and values. Culturally proficient instructors examine their own biases, expectations, and views of other cultures. They know that they must be aware of any limitations they have developed so that they can put these limitations aside when working with learners who differ from them. They also know that even when learners look like them, they cannot assume that the cultural similarities go beyond appearances.

REFLECT

What new cultural groups have you encountered in the recent past? How well did you know the culture? What prepared you to interact with people from the culture? What more would you like to have known? What do you still want to know about the culture?

_____

_____

_____

_____

Learning about the culture of your organization involves what Argyris (1990) describes as "double-loop learning." In *single-loop learning,* you identify a problem, identify alternative solutions, and take action. In *double-loop learning,* you become a student of your own culture, both individually and organizationally. You identify a problem, identify alternative solutions, select alternatives based on the organization's core values or beliefs, implement the solution, monitor the implementation, gather data, compare the data with the core values, modify solutions as needed, and continue the process. In essence, you not only strive for a solution, but you also want to match solutions to your core values. You develop a high value for data-driven strategies, benchmarks pegged to your core values and beliefs, and you accept no excuses for poor performance.

> Al Hernandez, Rose Diaz-Harris, Charlene Brennaman, and Ed Gonzales are meeting to discuss the work of the district's technology and diversity committees. Their common concern is the inequitable distribution of resources. Charlene begins the conversation: "I think what we need to do is survey what hardware and software technology we currently have in the schools, find out which kids are using it, brainstorm a variety of solutions for making better use of what we have, compare those solutions with our criteria, and implement the most viable solution. Within a year or two, we should have some good results."
>
> Rose responds, "You know, your idea is good, but I am concerned that it doesn't go deep enough. It seems to me that we need to know more about our current practice. For instance, I am interested to know which teachers and counselors use technology, how they use technology, what their training needs are, and how they view their students' skill levels."
>
> With this response, Rose was taking the discussion to a deeper level. She was prompting them to think about the culture of the school as to how technology was viewed and valued and who needed what levels of training—all this before developing a plan for acquisition of hardware and software.
>
> Al and Ed nod in agreement with Rose's suggestion. Ed says, "Yes, that makes sense, and it will allow us to more effectively implement the plan when we know people's needs."
>
> Al continues: "I can see the value of this approach. This way we will be able to determine who values the use of technology. I certainly don't want to see machines sitting unused in classrooms. It's important that we help our colleagues to see how the use of technology supports our instructional goals. Also, I would like to push our thinking. I'm interested to find out the demographics of students' use of technology."
>
> Charlene says, "I am not sure I follow you."
>
> "I think it's important to gather data on which courses are using technology and to get a profile of student use. My hunch is that students from the East Side of the community are exposed to far less use of technology in their classes. In fact, I would go so far as to guess that when they use computers, it's for drill lessons."

In gathering data on each of these concerns, the members of these committees will get a more complete look at the culture of their school. This is not to be constructed as a "gotcha" exercise, but as a realistic look at current practice. With these data, the educators, students, and members of the community can make informed decisions about these curricular-related issues.

One sure way to gather relevant information about your organization is to ask various constituent groups about their experiences with it. Learning how people experience the organization does two important things. First, it provides the organization with valuable data on successes and areas of needed improvement. Second, it honors the respondents by acknowledging that they have something to teach as well. Both the organization and the members of the new culture assume the roles of teacher and learner.

REFLECT

Focus on a learner in your classroom who is from a culture about which you know little. What questions do you have about how this person learns best? What do you know about this person's cultural values regarding learning? What do you know about the recent history of this learner's people? What would you like to know from this learner about her or his experiences in your classroom, in your school, or in your organization? Take a few minutes and jot down your responses or reactions to these questions. Perhaps you want to list additional questions you have.

_____

_____

_____

_____

In the study of culture, the topic of organizational culture is sometimes overlooked. Schein (1989) and others have helped us to see that organizations indeed have distinct cultures. Through the study of your organization, you can learn many valuable things, such as how the expressed values of the organization (e.g., a school district) may differ from the values perceived by the learners served by the organization. For example, you may see in a school's mission statement or statement of core values the words, "All children can learn." On examination of the achievement data, however, you learn that a significant portion of children are not learning. Consequently, you know a disconnect exists between what is said and what is done. Argyris (1990) describes this as the difference between espoused theory and theory in use. The conflict between espoused theory and theory in use is prevalent within schools that have significant numbers of students from low-income backgrounds or from communities of color.

Al Hernandez, speaking to members of the Diversity Committee, says, "The key words here are demographics and diversity. Take note of our reading in Reeves [2000]. Listen to these two comments that I pulled from reflection papers: 'Given the diversity of our community, these kids are doing pretty well.' 'For our demographics, I am pleased with how well our students are doing. In reality, they are getting an awful lot out of the cards they were dealt.'"

"What I see here, people," Al says, "is what Reeves called 'code words' or using academic language as epithets. This does not reflect much cultural competence in your roles as instructors."

REFLECT

Which groups of learners in your classroom are not performing as well as they should be? List the words used to describe them. How does this list compare with the sentiment in your organization's mission statement or core values? What meaning does this have for you?

_____

_____

_____

_____

A PROCESS, NOT AN EVENT

Often, when we are teaching about Cultural Proficiency, some people want to be "certified" as culturally competent or proficient. That does not surprise us—who would not want to be certified culturally proficient? As we work to become culturally proficient and struggle to institutionalize cultural knowledge, the focus must be on lifelong learning. The road to Cultural Proficiency is a lifelong journey because there is so much to learn. Institutionalizing the process of learning removes it from the realm of the special occasion and places it among things as basic and as important as brushing one's teeth.

When institutionalizing cultural knowledge as an instructor, you have both formal and informal learning opportunities. You can take classes and attend workshops. You also can learn about yourself, your organization, and others in less formal settings. By taking advantage of teachable moments, you will learn about and practice appropriate behaviors as you ask questions of others, respond to inquiries, and volunteer information about your culture and the culture of your school or other organization. The organization that institutionalizes Cultural Proficiency continuously examines its policies and practices, and it manifests in its policy and practice an in-depth understanding of the organization's culture and the culture of the individuals within it.

REFLECT

With a small group of your colleagues, describe in detail the unwritten rules of your school or organization. What are the stated values and what are the actualized values? How often do your core values conflict with those of your organization?

_____

_____

_____

_____

You have read this book because you want to be a culturally proficient instructor. We started with an invitation, and we end with a challenge. We invited you to think, observe, and reflect. We now challenge you to act. You now have the tools and the knowledge to assess your own behaviors and those of your organization within the context of Cultural Proficiency.

In the first six chapters, you learned basic terminology, the barriers to Cultural Proficiency, and about the Cultural Proficiency continuum. The next five chapters provided you with information about the essential elements of Cultural Proficiency. These elements are the competencies or standards by which organizations and the people in them plan for change and measure their accomplishments. When integrated into organizational policies and individual values, the essential elements become the standard practice, rather than isolated events or individual behaviors. People and their organizations become culturally proficient when specific strategies and behaviors are practiced consistently.

As we have walked with other instructors on the road to Cultural Proficiency, we have noticed that they predictably move through five levels of preparation: awareness, assimilation, processing, development, and deconstruction. If you have read this far, you have completed the first level. You are aware. You have become a student of your own reaction to people, organizations, and the issues that arise from diversity. Your reactions are clues to continued, deeper learning.

Many people assume that Cultural Proficiency is a process for learning about others. By now, you know that Cultural Proficiency involves primarily learning about yourself and your organization. That is why we call it an inside-out approach to diversity. It starts with the self. At the same time, even as you read this book, you have acquired additional facts and information that will help you in understanding the differences between yourself and others. This learning must continue. As a culturally proficient instructor, you will seek out information about the people you teach. You will integrate into your subject matter material information about the history, culture, and sociohistorical context of the people you work with.

One of the hardest tasks to complete as you move toward Cultural Proficiency is the processing of your own issues regarding power and oppression. As you completed the activities in this book and spent time with the reflect questions, you also were processing your feelings, acknowledging your biases and prejudices, and drawing new conclusions about who you are and who you can be. As an instructor, it is important you remember that oppression and power imbalances create obstacles for some people that do not exist for others. Developing the capacity to confront your own issues with power and oppression enables you to recognize these issues and neutralize them in your classroom.

In addition to whatever training you received to be an instructor, you need specific skills and techniques to manage the dynamics of difference and to facilitate effective cross-cultural communication in your classroom. Some very important steps include developing facilitation skills to foster healthy communication, to encourage critical reflection by your learners, and to engage with the learners as a community of practice. You can do this by watching others who are skilled, by taking workshops on advanced facilitation skills, and by practicing.

As you continue to reflect on your teaching practices—realizing that what was effective with one group of learners may not be successful with others—you will decide to stop doing some things and to change others. This process is called *deconstruction and reconstruction.* You want to *deconstruct*, assessing and examining what you do, and then you want to *reconstruct*, reordering or restructuring your craft of teaching practices. When you experience frustration and failure, having the capacity to check yourself and your delivery systems for what did not work and being receptive to learning different strategies shows that you are a reflective practitioner of your craft.

In planning your content and delivery systems, several considerations will improve your effectiveness in a diverse classroom. You may want to consider some of the following approaches as you work on your craft:

- Team teach so that you can have a mentor or be a mentor.
- Establish a process for sharing activities and incidents throughout the course of instruction. The classroom experience is most vivid when learners can relate in-classroom learning to their lives outside the classroom and when you can critically reflect on what they do with others outside the classroom.
- Engage in strategic, systematic coaching with your colleagues.
- Hold a retreat for yourself and other instructors to deal with *your and their* issues of oppression and power so that you and they are more comfortable and better prepared to facilitate classroom discussions.
- Obtain instruction on how to infuse issues of diversity into your classes and how to respond to learner statements of bias and injustice. You do not have to have all the answers, but you must be comfortable fielding the questions.
- Learn not to be afraid to recognize your mistakes. Acknowledge them, learn from them, and redirect them to more effective actions.
- Develop a process for mentoring, coaching, and collecting ideas. One of the most invaluable resources for instructors is the successful experience of colleagues.

Mentors and apprentices are partners in an ancient human dance, and one of teaching's great rewards is the daily chance it gives us to get back on the dance floor. It is the dance of the spiraling generations, in which the old empower the young with their experience and the young empower the old with new life, reweaving the fabric of the human community as they touch and turn (Parker Palmer in Sennett, p. 19).

REFLECT

What will be your next steps?

_____

_____

_____

_____

ENGAGE

Compile a list of teaching practices you consider to be particularly effective. With a group of your colleagues, analyze the relationship between your list of teaching practices and the essential elements of Cultural Proficiency.

_____

_____

_____

_____

WHAT DIFFERENCE DO YOU MAKE?

By completing the preceding Engage activity, you have gained immediate evidence that a community of practice is useful and makes a difference. Moreover, if you are committed to becoming a culturally proficient instructor, you probably have already begun to think of the people with whom you can work to make a difference. In your community of practice, you will learn and grow together as you create nurturing, supportive, growth-producing environments for the learners in your classroom.

REFLECT

What difference do you make with others in your community of practice?

_____

_____

_____

_____

> Maple View's Superintendent, Dr. Sandra Patton had been asked to address the newest group that had completed the Leadership Maple View program. She had talked with them about her favorite topic, Cultural Proficiency, and was reassuring them that they could indeed make a difference.
>
> "Each of us has one little pebble of influence," she says. "Now you can take that pebble and stick it in your pocket or drop it into your purse, and you are right—nothing will change. You could take your one little pebble and drop it into the river. You may see a splash; it might hit a little fish on the head. But again, you won't see much change.
>
> "Another option for you is to join with the others here who also have pebbles, and together, you can make some strategic decisions. You could, for example, band together and decide that the river is not the best place for pebbles. For instance, at the lake, if you dropped all your pebbles at the same spot at the same time, you could make quite a splash.
>
> "Friends, as leaders of this city, you have already banded together, and the city of Maple View is the kind of pond where you can make a difference. Let us all pledge here tonight to drop our pebbles of Cultural Proficiency into our Maple View pond. Each of us—at the schools, at the hospital, downtown, East Side, and West Side—together, we will make a big difference."

GO DEEPER

What will you do with your pebble of influence?

_____

_____

_____

_____

12

Your Action Plan

I think . . . of teachers who create the conditions under which young people must spend so many hours: some shine a light that allows new growth to flourish, while others cast a shadow under which seedlings die.

—Parker J. Palmer[1]

The extent to which we cast shadows or light is related to our personal journeys as educators and our level of commitment to our own learning, our advocacy, and our sense of social justice. Whether our role in education is that of teacher, administrator, or counselor, our sole purpose as an educator must be to provide and support high-quality instruction. High-quality instruction must have at least two outcomes: to narrow and close access and academic achievement gaps, and to prepare students to function in a diverse society and world. With this third edition of *Culturally Proficient Instruction: A Guide for People Who Teach,* we have endeavored to guide an *inside-out* journey for you to explore and probe your own values and behaviors and to examine and understand the policies and practices in your classroom and school that either impede or facilitate student engagement and success. The deeper understanding of ourselves and our schools prepares us to make choices in the best interest of our students.

URGENCY AND INTENTIONALITY

Throughout this book we have endeavored to paint a picture of urgency paired with hope. For many of our students, the situation is dire and their needs are immediate and complex. Many variables, external and internal to the school, are beyond our

---

[1]Palmer (2000), p. 78.

control as educators. Therefore, we must recognize the importance of our taking responsibility for the direct and intentional impact we have during the time students are in our classrooms and schools.

Assume for a moment that the students in your classroom or schools who are not meeting academic standards basic for success in modern society are your own children, brothers and sisters, nieces and nephews, or grandchildren. Do you feel the urgency now? Our approach, as you know by now, is described as an 'inside-out" process. This chapter guides you in articulating your inside-out Cultural Proficiency experiences into an action plan. We wish you well as you continue this journey for you and your school. This is a journey that your school leadership team may want to take with you to sustain culturally proficient educational initiatives.

THE INSIDE-OUT PROCESS IS FOR YOU, YOUR SCHOOL, AND YOUR COMMUNITY

This chapter is designed to help you develop a personal plan for yourself as an educator, whether teacher, administrator, or counselor. To this point in the book you have had the opportunity to:

- Reflect on your inside out process for learning about your own culture, the culture of your school, and the culture of the community you serve
- Reflect on your thinking and your practice.
- Read and study case stories from the Maple View School District.

In this chapter you are encouraged to review and summarize your learning and to determine how you want to function as a culturally proficient educator committed to access and equity for all students in your school.

CHAPTER 7: ASSESS CULTURE

To summarize your learning about the essential element and its relationship to your role of teacher, or as an administrator or counselor in support of teachers, you are guided through a three-step review and summary process as the initial step in designing your action plan.

Step 1: Inside-Out Process. Take a few moments and peruse Chapter 7, paying particular attention to your responses to the reflective inside-out learning processes. Review your entries and synthesize two reflections that represent the inside-out process relative to you, your school, and the community your school serves. Summarize your learning in the space below.

_____

_____

_____

_____

_____

_____

Step 2: Case Stories. This time browse through the Chapter 7 stories and summarize one or two key ideas you glean from reading the stories again. Use the space below to summarize those key ideas.

_____

_____

_____

_____

_____

Step 3: Getting Centered and Going Deeper. Read your reflections to the Chapter 7 opening and closing activities, paying particular attention to your reactions and your observations of self and others. Use the space below to summarize key learning and insights.

_____

_____

_____

_____

_____

CHAPTER 8: VALUE DIVERSITY

This time you are invited to return to Chapter 8. Review and summarize your learning about the essential element and its relationship to your role as teacher, or administrator or counselor in support of teachers, through the three-step review and summary process as the next step in developing your action plan.

Step 1: Inside-Out Process. Return to Chapter 8, paying particular attention to your responses to the reflective inside-out learning processes. Reread your recordings and synthesize two reflections that represent your inside-out process relative to you, your school, and the community your school serves. The space below is provided for you to summarize your learning.

_____

_____

_____

_____

_____

_____

Step 2: Case Stories. Review the Chapter 8 stories and summarize one or two key ideas you take from the stories. Use the space below to summarize those key ideas.

_____

_____

_____

_____

_____

_____

Step 3: Getting Centered and Going Deeper. Read your reflections to the Chapter 8 opening and closing activities. As you read, take note of any feelings that may surface for you and your observations of self and others. The space below is to summarize key learning and insights.

_____

_____

_____

_____

_____

_____

CHAPTER 9: MANAGE THE DYNAMICS OF DIFFERENCE

By continuing this three-step review and summary process, you will progress in the development of a personal action plan. Be intentional in following the prompts, in particular, paying attention to your thoughts and reactions as they arise.

Step 1: Inside-Out Process. Revisit Chapter 9, focusing attention to your responses to the reflective inside-out learning processes. Review your entries and synthesize two reflections that represent your inside-out process relative to you, your school, and the community your school serves. Summarize your learning in the space below.

_____

_____

_____

_____

_____

Step 2: Case Stories. Now, take a few moments and browse the Chapter 9 stories and summarize one or two key ideas that emerge from reading the stories again. Use the space below to summarize those key ideas.

_____

_____

_____

_____

_____

Step 3: Getting Centered and Going Deeper. Your reflections to the opening and closing activities may evoke certain reactions and observations about yourself and others. Use the space below to summarize reactions, learning, and insights.

_____

_____

_____

_____

_____

CHAPTER 10: ADAPT TO DIVERSITY

You are now very familiar with three-step review and summary process provided to support you in designing your action plan. Take your time and enjoy your journey of continuous self-discovery.

Step 1: Inside-Out Process. Take another look at Chapter 10, rereading your responses to the reflective inside-out learning processes. Construct two reflections prompted in this reread that represent the inside-out process relative to you, your school, and the community your school serves. Use the space below to summarize your thinking.

_____

_____

_____

_____

_____

_____

Step 2: Case Stories. Summarize one or two key ideas you gather from reading the Chapter 10 stories again. Use the space below to summarize those key ideas.

_____

_____

_____

_____

_____

_____

Step 3: Getting Centered and Going Deeper. Be mindful of your reactions and observations of self and others as you reread your reflections to the Chapter 10 opening and closing activities. The space below is for you to summarize key learning and insights.

_____

_____

_____

_____

_____

_____

CHAPTER 11: INSTITUTIONALIZE CULTURAL KNOWLEDGE

This is the final three-step review to summarize learning about an essential element, and its relationship to the role of school counselor, to be used in designing your action plan. Note the manner in which your responses begin to knit together your observations and provide you guidance for making commitments for yourself and your students.

Step 1: Inside-Out Process. Look through Chapter 11, attending to your responses to the reflective inside-out learning processes. Review your entries and synthesize two reflections that represent your inside-out process relative to you, your school, and the community your school serves. Summarize your learning in the space below.

_____

_____

_____

_____

_____

_____

Step 2: Case Stories. Take a few moments to look through the Chapter 11 stories one more time, and then summarize one or two key ideas you glean from reading the stories again. The space below is for you to summarize those key ideas.

_____

_____

_____

_____

_____

_____

Step 3: Getting Centered and Going Deeper. Reread your reflections to Chapter 11's opening and closing activities. What do you notice about your reactions and your observations of self and others? Use the space below to summarize key learning and insights.

_____

_____

_____

_____

_____

FROM WORDS TO ACTION

STEPS FOR PROVIDING EQUITY

1. Use the space below to summarize your reactions and feelings to the reading and reflective activities in Chapters 7–11. Your summary may consist of key words or you may choose a longer, expository approach.

_____

_____

_____

_____

_____

2. As you read and analyze what you have written, what insights do you have about yourself as an teacher, or an administrator or counselor supporting teachers, working in a diverse setting to provide access and equitable opportunity to students?

_____

_____

_____

_____

_____

_____

3. In what ways does the inside-out approach of Cultural Proficiency contribute to learning about yourself?

_____

_____

_____

_____

_____

4. In what ways does the inside-out approach contribute to learning about the culture of your school?

_____

_____

_____

_____

_____

5. In what ways does the inside-out approach contribute to learning about the community your school serves?

_____

_____

_____

_____

6. Now that you know what you know, what three commitments are you willing to make to be an advocate for equity in your school?

_____

_____

_____

_____

7. In what ways will you, as a teacher, support equity in your school? If you are an administrator or counselor, in what ways will you work with your teachers to support equity in your school? What three bold steps will you take within the next three to six months to demonstrate your commitments?

_____

_____

_____

_____

It is up to you and your colleagues to craft sustainable steps to a culturally proficient educational environment for you and your students. For our preK–12 schools to serve our diverse society in ways that are equitable and to meet the twenty-first century needs of a democracy requires the will and skill of all educators. In this book we have focused on teachers, as well as administrators and counselors who support teachers, to address issues of equity and inequity rooted in historical and prevalent forces. These forces are not immutable; they can be confronted and circumvented. Within each of us is the potential moral commitment that can give rise to voices of hope and desire. Each of us must move toward action in our schools and communities. Now that you know the urgency, to what actions are you willing to commit?

References and Recommended Reading

American Association of Colleges of Teacher Education. (2010). *21st century knowledge and skills in educator preparation.* Washington, DC: Author.

Andrews, William L., & Henry Louis Gates, Jr. (1999). *The civitas anthology of African American slave narratives.* Washington, DC: Counterpoint.

Argyris, Chris. (1990). *Overcoming organizational defenses.* Boston: Allyn & Bacon.

Armstrong, David A., Kenneth T. Henson, & Tom V. Savage. (2005). *Teaching today: An introduction to education* (7th ed.). Upper Saddle River, NJ: Pearson.

Baker, C. (2011). *Foundations of bilingual education and bilingualism* (5th ed.). Clevedon, Avon, UK: Multilingual Matters.

Ball, Edward. (1998). *Slaves in the family.* New York: Ballantine.

Banks, James A. (1999). *An introduction to multicultural education.* Needham Heights, MA: Allyn & Bacon.

Barker, Joel. (2000). *Wealth, innovation, and diversity: Putting our differences to work in the 21st century* [DVD]. Available from http://www.wealthinnovationanddiversity.com

Berliner, David C., & B. J. Biddle. (1996). *The manufactured crisis: Myths, fraud, and the attack on America's public schools.* Reading, MA: Addison-Wesley.

Bigelow, Bill, & Bob Peterson. (1998). *Rethinking Columbus: The next 500 years.* Milwaukee, WI: Rethinking Schools.

Boyer, Ernest. (1983). High school: A report on secondary education in America. New York: Harper & Row.

Bracey, Gerald. (2000). The 10th Bracey report on the condition of public education. *Phi Delta Kappan, 82*(2), 133–144.

Bridges, William. (2004). Transitions: Making sense of life's changes. Cambridge, MA: Da Capo Press.

Bridges, William. (2009). Managing transitions: Making the most of change. Cambridge, MA: Da Capo Lifelong Books.

Brown v. Board of Education of Topeka, 347 U.S. 483 (1954).

Buendia, Edward, Nancy Ares, Brenda Juarez, & Megan Peercy. (2004). The geographies of difference: The production of East Side, West Side, and Central City School. *American Educational Research Journal, 41*(4), 833–863.

Byrk, Anthony S., & Barbara Schneider. (2002). *Trust in schools: A core resource for improvement.* New York: Russell Sage Foundation.

Carmichael, Stokely, & Charles Hamilton. (1967). *Black power: The politics of liberation in America.* New York: Random House.

Chenoweth, Karin. (2007). *It's being done: Academic success in unexpected schools.* Cambridge, MA: Harvard University Press.

Coleman, James S., Earnest Q. Campbell, Carol J. Hobson, James McPartland, Alexander M. Mood, Frederick D. Weinfeld, & Robert L. York. (1966). *Equality of educational opportunity.* Washington, DC: Government Printing Office.

Cross, Terry, Barbara Bazron, Karl Dennis, & Mareasa Isaacs. (1989). *Toward a culturally competent system of care* (Vol. 1). Washington, DC: Georgetown University Child Development Program, Child and Adolescent Service System Program.

Cross, Terry, Barbara J. Bazron, Karl Dennis, & Mareasa R. Isaacs. (1993). *Toward a culturally competent system of care* (Vol. 2). Washington, DC: Georgetown University Child Development Program, Child and Adolescent Service System Program.

Darling-Hammond, Linda, & Deborah Loewenberg Ball. (1997). *Teaching for high standards: What policymakers need to know and be able to do.* Retrieved from http://govinfo.library.unt.edu/negp/Reports/highstds.htm

Delpit, Lisa. (1995). *Other people's children: Cultural conflict in the classroom.* New York: New Press.

Dewey, John. (1938). *Experience and education.* New York: Collier.

Education Trust. (2005). *The power to change: High schools that help all students to achieve.* Washington, DC: EdTrust.

Elementary and Secondary Education Act of 1965 (ESEA), Pub. L. No. 89-10, 79 Stat. 27 (1965).

Frankenberg, Erica, & Gary Orfield. (2006). *The segregation of American teachers.* Los Angeles: The Civil Rights Project, UCLA. Retrieved from http://civilrightsproject.ucla.edu/research/k-12-education/integration-and-diversity/the-segregation-of-american-teachers

Franklin, John Hope, & Alfred A. Moss, Jr. (1988). *From slavery to freedom: A history of Negro Americans* (6th ed.). New York: McGraw-Hill.

Freire, Paolo. (1987). *Pedagogy of the oppressed.* New York: Continuum.

Freire, Paulo. (1970). *Pedagogy of the oppressed.* New York: Continuum.

Freire, Paulo. (1998). *Pedagogy of freedom: Ethics, democracy, and civic courage.* New York: Rowman & Littlefield.

Freire, Paulo. (1999). *Pedagogy of the oppressed* (Rev. ed.). New York: Continuum.

Fuentes, Carlos. (1992). Hispanic USA: A mirror of others. *The Nation, 411*(12), 245.

Gabriel, John C. (2005). *How to thrive as a teacher leader.* Alexandria, VA: Association for Supervision and Curriculum Development.

Garmston, Robert, & Bruce Wellman. (2008). *Syllabus—the adaptive school: A sourcebook for developing collaborative groups* (5th ed.). Norwood, MA: Christopher-Gordon.

Glickman, Carl D. (2002). *Leadership for learning: How to help teachers succeed.* Alexandria, VA: Association for Supervision and Curriculum Development.

Gordon, Milton M. (1978). *Human nature, class, and ethnicity.* New York: Oxford University Press.

Grant, Carl A., & Christine E. Sleeter. (2007). *Doing multicultural education for achievement and equity.* New York: CRC Press.

Hall, Edward T. (1959). *The silent language.* New York: Doubleday.

Haycock, Kati. (1998). Good teaching matters: How well-qualified teachers can close the gap. *Thinking K–16: A Publication of the Education Trust, 3*(2), 1–16.

Hernandez, Hilda. (1999). *Teaching in multicultural classrooms.* Englewood Cliffs, NJ: Prentice-Hall.

Hord, Shirley M., & William L. Sommers. (2008). *Leading professional learning communities: Voices from research and practice.* Thousand Oaks, CA: Corwin.

Hoy, Anita W., & Wayne K. Hoy. (2009). *Instructional leadership: A research-based guide to learning in schools* (3rd ed.). Boston: Pearson.

Ito, Sasho. (1979). Review of minority education and caste: The American system in cross-cultural perspective. *Social Forces, 57*(3), 989–990.

Johnson, Ruth S. (2002) *Using data to close the achievement gap: How to measure equity in our schools.* Thousand Oaks, CA: Corwin.

Josephy, Alvin M., Jr. (Ed.). (1991). *America in 1492: The world of Indian peoples before the arrival of Columbus.* New York: Vintage.

Karns, Michelle. (1998). *Ethnic barriers and biases: How to become an agent for change.* Sebastopol, CA: National Training Associates.

Kellner-Rogers, Myron. (1996). *A simpler way.* San Francisco: Barrett-Koehler.

Kent, Karen. (1999). Teachers developing as professionals. In *California field guide for teachers' professional development: Designs for learning.* Sacramento: California Department of Education.

Kobrin, David. (2004). *In there with the kids: Crafting lessons that connect with students* (2nd ed.). Alexandria, VA: Association for Supervision and Curriculum Development.

Kozol, Jonathan. (2007). *Letters to a young teacher.* New York: Crown.

Kunzig, Robert. (2011). Find out why you shouldn't panic—at least, not yet. *National Geographic, 219*(1), 32–69.

Lawson, Michael A. (2003). School-family relations in context: Parent and teacher perceptions of parent involvement. *Urban Education, 38*(1), 77–133.

Lindsey, Delores B. (1999). Evidence of engagement: A study of CSLA's ventures leadership training program participants' engagement of teachers in creating an environment for powerful learning [CD-ROM]. Abstract retrieved from ProQuest File (Dissertation Abstracts Item No. 9956040)

Lindsey, Delores B. (2000, September). *Spotlight on teaching.* Paper presented at the Orange Unified School District Staff Development Day, Orange, CA.

Lindsey, Delores B., Linda D. Jungwirth, Jarvis V.N.C. Pahl, & Randall B. Lindsey. (2009). *Culturally proficient learning communities: Confronting inequities through collaborative curiosity.* Thousand Oaks, CA: Corwin.

Lindsey, Randall B., Michelle S. Karns, & Keith Myatt. (2010). *Culturally proficient education: An assets-based approach to conditions of poverty.* Thousand Oaks, CA: Corwin.

Lindsey, Randall B., Kikanza Nuri-Robins, & Raymond D. Terrell. (1999). *Cultural proficiency: A manual for school leaders.* Thousand Oaks, CA: Corwin.

Lindsey, Randall B., Kikanza Nuri-Robins, & Raymond D. Terrell. (2009). *Cultural proficiency: A manual for school leaders* (3rd ed.). Thousand Oaks, CA: Corwin.

Loewen, James W. (1995). *Lies my teacher told me: Everything your American history textbook got wrong.* New York: New Press.

Marzano, Robert J., Debra J. Pickering, & Jane F. Pollock. (2001). *Classroom instruction that works: Research-based strategies for increasing student achievement.* Alexandria, VA: Association for Supervision and Curriculum Development.

McAllister, Gretchen, & Jacqueline Jordan Irvine. (2000). Cross-cultural competency and multicultural teacher education. *Review of Educational Research, 70*(1), 3–24.

McIntyre, Alice M. (1997). *Making meaning of whiteness: Exploring racial identity with white teachers.* Albany: State University of New York Press.

Mithun, Jacqueline. (1979). Minority education and caste: The American system in cross-cultural perspective. *American Anthropologist, 81*(3), 694–695.

Murray, Carolyn B., & Halford H. Fairchild. (1989). Models of black adolescent academic underachievement. In Reginald L. Jones (Ed.), *Black adolescents* (pp. 229–245). Berkeley, CA: Cobb & Henry.

Myrdal, Gunnar. (1944). *An American dilemma* (Vol. 11). New York: Pantheon.

Naisbitt, John, & Patricia Aburdene. (1990). *Megatrends 2000: Ten new trends for the 1990s.* New York: William Morrow.

National Study Group for the Affirmative Development of Academic Ability. (2004). *All students reaching the top: Strategies for closing academic gaps.* Naperville, IL: North Central Regional Educational Laboratory, Learning Point Associates.

Nieto, Sonia. (1999a). *Affirming diversity: The sociopolitical context of multicultural education.* New York: Longman.

Nieto, Sonia. (1999b). *The light in their eyes: Creating multicultural learning communities.* New York: Teachers College Press.

No Child Left Behind Act of 2001 (NCLB), Pub. L. No. 107-110, 115 Stat. 1425 (2002).

Noguera, Pedro. (1999). *Equity in education: What difference can teachers make?* Sacramento: California State Department of Education, California Professional Development Consortia.

Oakes, Jeannie. (2004, April). *Schools that shock the conscience: What Williams v. California reveals about research and the struggle for education on equal terms 50 years after Brown.* Distinguished lecture given at the annual meeting of the American Educational research Association in San Diego, CA.

Obama, Barack. (2006). *The audacity of hope.* New York: Three Rivers Press.

Ogbu, John. (1978). *Minority education and caste: The American system in cross-cultural perspective.* New York: Academic Press.

Owens, Robert G. (1995). *Organizational behavior in education.* Boston: Allyn & Bacon.

Public Schools Accountability Act of 1999 (PSAA), Pub. L. 106-400, 114 Stat. 1675 (2000).

Palmer, Parker J. (1998). *The courage to teach: Exploring the inner landscape of a teacher's life.* San Francisco: Jossey-Bass.

Palmer, Parker J. (2000). *Let your life speak: Listening for the voice of vocation.* San Francisco: Jossey-Bass.

Pappano, Laura. (2010). *Inside school turnarounds: Urgent hopes, unfolding stories.* Cambridge, MA: Harvard Education Press.

Pearl, Arthurm, & Tony Knight. (1999). *The democratic classroom: Theory to inform practice.* Cresskill, NJ: Hampton Press.

Perie, Marianne, Rebecca Moran, & Anthony D. Lutkus. (2005). *NAEP 2004 trends in academic progress three decades of student performance in reading and mathematics.* Washington, DC: U.S. Department of Education. Retrieved from http: //nces.ed.gov/pubsearch/pubsinfo.asp?pubid2005464

Perspectives on education in America: Hearing before Subcommittee on Elementary, Secondary, and Vocational Education, Committee on Education and Labor, House of Representatives, 102d Cong. 175 (1991) (testimony of Michael A. Wartell and Robert M. Huelskamp, Sandia National Laboratories).

Plessy v. Ferguson, 163 U.S. 537 (1896).

Popham, James W. (2008). *Transformative assessment.* Alexandria, VA: Association for Supervision and Curriculum Development.

Powers, Jeanne M. (2004). High-stakes accountability and equity: Using evidence from California's Public Schools Accountability Act to address the issues in *Williams v. State of California. American Educational Research Journal, 41*(4), 763–795.

Ravitch, Diane. (2010). *The death and life of the great American school system: How testing and choice are undermining education.* New York: Basic Books.

Reeves, Douglas B. (2000). *Accountability in action: A blueprint for learning organizations.* Denver: Center for Performance Assessment.

Reyes, Pedro, Jay D. Scribner, & Alicia P. Scribner. (1999). *Lessons from high-performing Hispanic schools: Creating learning communities.* New York: Teachers College Press.

Riehl, Carolyn J. (2000). The principal's role in creating inclusive schools for diverse students: A review of normative, empirical, and critical literature on the practice of educational administration. *Review of Educational Research, 70*(1), 55–81.

Rist, Ray. (1979). *Desegregated schools: Appraisal of an American experiment.* New York: Basic Books.

Rosenholtz, Susan J. (1991). *Teachers' workplace: The social organization of schools.* New York: Teachers College Press.

Santamaria, Lorri J. (2009). Culturally responsive differentiated instruction: Narrowing gaps between best pedagogical practices benefiting all learners. *Teachers College Record, 111*(1), 214–247. Retrieved from http://www.tcrecord.org (ID Number: 15210)

Satir, Virginia. (1972). *People making.* Palo Alto, CA: Science & Behavior Books.

Schein, Edgar. (1989). *Organizational culture and leadership: A dynamic view.* San Francisco: Jossey-Bass.

Senge, Peter, Nelda Cambron-McCabe, Timothy Lucas, Bryan Smith, James Dutton, & Art Kleiner. (2000). *Schools that learn: A fifth discipline fieldbook for educators, parents, and everyone who cares about education.* New York: Doubleday.

Senge, Peter, Art Kleiner, Charlotte Roberts, Richard B.Ross, & Bryan S. Smith. (1994). *The fifth discipline fieldbook: Strategies and tools for building a learning organization.* New York: Doubleday.

Senge, Peter, Art Kleiner, Charlotte Roberts, George Roth, Richard B. Ross, & Bryan S. Smith. (1999). *The dance of change.* New York: Doubleday.

Sennett, Frank. (2004). *400 quotable quotes from the world's leading educators.* Thousand Oaks, CA: Corwin.

Sergiovanni, Thomas J. (1994). *Building community in schools.* San Francisco: Jossey-Bass.

Singham, Mano. (1998). The canary in the mine. *Phi Delta Kappan, 80*(1), 9–15.

Sleeter, Christine E., & Carl A. Grant. (1994). *Making choices for multicultural education: Five approaches to race.* New York: Merrill.

Strong, Richard W., Harvey F. Silver, & Matthew J. Perini. (2001). *Teaching what matters most: Standards and strategies for raising student achievement.* Alexandria, VA: Association for Supervision and Curriculum Development.

Sue, Derald Wing. (2010). *Microaggressions in everyday life: Race, gender, and sexual orientation.* Hoboken, NJ: John Wiley.

Takaki, Ronald. (1993). *A different mirror: A history of multicultural America.* Boston: Little, Brown.

Thomas, Kenneth, & Ralph H. Kilmann. (1974). *Conflict mode instrument.* Tuxedo, NY: Xicom.

Thompson, Gail L. (2007). *Up where we belong: Helping African American and Latino students rise in school and in life*. San Francisco: Jossey-Bass.

Tomlinson, Carol Ann. (1999). *The differentiated classroom: Responding to the needs of all learners*. Alexandria, VA: Association for Supervision and Curriculum Development.

U.S. Department of Education (2009). *The condition of education 2009*. (NCES 2009–08) Alexandria, VA: National Center for Education Statistics.

Ury, William. (1991). *Getting past no: Negotiating with difficult people*. New York: Bantam.

Vigil, James Diego. (1980). *From Indians to Chicanos: A sociocultural history*. St. Louis, MO: Mosby.

Villa, Richard A., & Jacqueline S. Thousand. (2005). *Creating an inclusive school* (2nd ed.). Alexandria, VA: Association for Supervision and Curriculum Development.

Voltz, Deborah L., Michele Jean Sims, & Betty Nelson. (2010). *Connecting teachers, students and standards: Strategies for success in diverse and inclusive classrooms*. Alexandria, VA: Association for Supervision and Curriculum Development.

Wenger, Etienne. (1998). *Communities of practice: Learning, meaning and identity*. New York: Cambridge University Press.

Wheatley, Margaret J. (1994). *Leadership and the new science*. San Francisco: Berrett-Koehler.

Wheatley, Margaret J., & Myron Kellner-Rogers, (Technical Advisers), Peter J. Jordan (Executive Producer). (1995). *Lessons from the new workplace* [VHS]. Carlsbad, CA: CRM Films.

Williams, Eliezer, et al. v. State of California et al., 34 Cal. 3d 18. (2004).

Wilmore, Elaine L. (2002). *Principal leadership: Applying the new educational leadership constituent council (ELCC) standards*. Thousand Oaks, CA: Corwin.

Index

Aburdene, P., 182
Accommodation, 141
Accomplished instructors, 42–43
Achievement gap, 16
Achievement standards, 26–29, 30–31, 37
Action plan, 169–179
Adaptability, 5, 59, 61–62, 144–158, 174–175
Agents/agent groups, 63–64
American Association of Colleges of Teacher Education, 27, 31
Andrews, W. L., 81
Anger, 67
Ares, N. *see* Buendia, E.
Argyris, C., 161, 163
Armstrong, D. A., 26, 27, 32, 33
Assessment barriers, 71, 74
Assessment, cultural, 102–115, 170–171
Assumptions, 60–61

Baker, C., viii
Ball, D. L., xxvi
Ball, E., 66–67
Banks, J. A., 34, 134
Barker, J., 33
Barriers, 5–6, 7, 58–75
Bazron, B., xviii
Belief systems, 34–35, 60–61
Berliner, D. C., 180
Bias, 60–61
Biddle, B. J., 180
Bigelow, B., 180
Blindness, cultural, 4, 87–90, 98, 99
Boyer, E., 88
Bracey, G., 180
Bridges, W., 61–62
Brown v. Board of Education of Topeka (1954), x
Buendia, E., 41
Bullies, 64, 151
Byrk, A. S., 33

California Professional Standards for Education Administration (CPSELs), 26
California Professional Teaching Standards (CSTPs), 26
Cambron-McCabe, N. *see* Senge, P.
Campbell, E. Q., 180
Carmichael, S., 81
Castelike minority groups, 66, 69
Centering activities
  barriers, 58
  change processes, 144
  conflict management, 131
  cultural knowledge, 159
  inappropriate behavior, 76
  learning styles, 102
  local communities, 19–20
  marginalized students, 2
  standards, 25
  teaching philosophy, 40–41
  value systems, 116
Change processes, 61–62, 144–158, 174–175
Chenoweth, K., 70
Chomsky, N., 58
Class lines, 50
Clay, M. M., 144
Coleman, J. S., 180
Collaboration, 125–127, 142
Commitment to change, 146–158
Common Core State Standards (CCSSs), 26–27
Communities of practice, 157–158, 167–168
Communitycentric, 53
Community perceptions, 114
Competence, cultural, 94–97, 98, 100
Competition, 142
Compromise, 141–142
Conflict management, 131–143, 151, 173–174
Content barriers, 71, 73

Continuum model
  benefits, 76–79
  characteristics, 4–5, 7
  cultural blindness, 4, 87–90, 98, 99
  cultural competence, 94–97, 98, 100
  cultural destructiveness, 4, 79–83, 98, 99
  cultural incapacity, 4, 83–87, 98, 99
  cultural precompetence, 5, 90–94, 98, 99
  cultural proficiency, 5, 97–98, 100
Corporate cultures, 13
Courageous conversations, 152–155
Cross, T., xviii, 3, 131
Cultural assessment, 102–115, 170–171
Cultural competence, 56–57
Cultural differences, 137, 139
Cultural diversity, 49–51
Cultural expectations, 45–47
Cultural identity, 13–14, 44–46, 111
Cultural influences, 32
Cultural knowledge, 159–167, 176–177
Culturally and linguistically diverse (CLD)
    students, viii–xi
Culturally defined needs, 51–52
Culturally proficient instruction, 16
Culturally proficient instructors
  change processes, 150–151
  characteristics, 36
  collaboration, 125–127
  cultural knowledge, 160–163, 164
  diversity-valuing behaviors, 118–120,
      122, 172–173
  institutional barriers, 70–75
  learning strategies, 165–167
  learning styles, 105–108
  organizational culture, 111–114
  personal action plan, 169–179
Cultural perception activity, 17–18
Cultural proficiency see also Essential elements
  barriers, 5–6, 7, 58–75
  basic tools, 3–8
  benefits, 8–9
  characteristics, 3–4
  continuum model, 4–5, 7, 76–100
  definition, 15–16
  guiding principles, 4, 7, 43–44
  hidden curriculum, 32–34

Darling-Hammond, L., xxvi
Debriefing questions, 154–155
Deconstruction and reconstruction
    process, 166
Delivery barriers, 71, 73
Delpit, L., 181
Democratic pedagogy, x

Dennis, K., xviii
Destructiveness, cultural, 4, 79–83, 98, 99
de Tocqueville, A., 67
Dewey, J., 19
Dialogue, 16
Differences and similarities, 116–118,
    127–130
Differentiated instruction, 51
Dignity, 52
Discrimination, 15
Disempowerment, 83
Diverse thought patterns, 55–56
Diversity, definition of, 15
Diversity-valuing behaviors
  collaboration, 125–127
  differences and similarities, 116–118,
      127–130
  intentionality, 118–122
  personal action plan, 172–173
  respectfulness, 122–125
Dominant cultures, 43–51, 62–64, 66–70
Double-loop learning, 161–162
Dutton, J. see Senge, P.

Educational impact, 167–168
Education Trust, 31
Effective instructors, 58–60
Elementary and Secondary Education
    Act (1965), 26
Engagement activities
  conflict management, 143
  cultural blindness, 89–90
  cultural perceptions, 17–18
  debriefing questions, 155
  individual cultural assessment, 108–109
  institutional barriers, 72, 73–75
  instructional strategies, 156, 167
  learner performance, 122
  social encounter experiences, 9–12
  terminology, 14–17
Entitlement, 6, 58–59, 63, 69, 72
Equality, 14, 88
Equity, 14, 88
Espoused theory versus theory in use, 163
Essential elements
  change processes, 144–158, 174–175
  characteristics, 6, 7
  conflict management, 131–143, 173–174
  cultural assessment, 101–115, 170–171
  diversity-valuing behaviors, 116–130,
      172–173
  foundational standards, 35–36
  institutionalized cultural knowledge,
      159–167, 176–177

Ethnic cultures, 13
European immigrant groups, 66
Expectation barriers, 71, 74
Experienced instructors, 42–43

Facts, 135, 139
Fairchild, H. H., 182
Family involvement, 53–55
Frankenberg, E., ix
Franklin, J. H., 81
Freire, P., x, 83
Fuentes, C., x
Fullan, M., 159

Gabriel, J. C., 181
Garmston, R., 181
Gates, H. L., Jr., 81
Geographical differences, 41
Glickman, C. D., 181
Gordon, M. M., 181
Grant, C. A., 29
Groupness, 13–14, 44
Guiding principles, 4, 7, 43–44
Guilt, 67

Hall, E. T., 181
Hamilton, C., 81
Haycock, K., xxvi, 31
Henson, K. T., 26, 27, 32, 33
Hernandez, H., 181
Hidden curriculum, 32–34
High-quality instruction, xxvi–xxvii
Historical racism, 80
Hobson, C. J., 180
Hord, S. M., 181
Houston, P. D., 116
Hoy, A. W., 31
Hoy, W. K., 31

Inappropriate behavior, 76
Incapacity, cultural, 4, 83–87, 98, 99
Inclusive language and materials, 155–156
Individual cultural assessment, 108–111
Influential instructors, 41–43
Information-gathering strategies, 161–163
Inner curriculum, 32–33
Inside-out action plan, 170–179
Institutional barriers, 70–75
Institutionalized cultural knowledge,
    159–167, 176–177
Instructional strategies, 102–108, 167
Instruction quality, 41
INTASC Model Core Standards, 26
Intentional community of practice, 157

Intentionality, 118–122, 146, 152, 169–170
Internalized oppression, 83
Interstate New Instructor Assessment and
    Support Consortium, 26
Isaacs, M., xviii
Ito, S., 66

Johnson, R. S., 31, 34
Jordan Irvine, J., 134
Jordan, P. J. see Wheatley, M. J.
Josephy, A. M., Jr., 181
Juarez, B. see Buendia, E.
Jungwirth, L. D., 28

Karns, M. S., 181
Kellner-Rogers, M., 152
Kent, K., 42
Kilmann, R. H., 142
Kleiner, A., 152
Knight, T., ix
Kobrin, D., 182
Kozol, J., 182
Kunzig, R., viii

Ladson-Billings, G., 40
Language barriers, 69–70
Lawson, M. A., 53
Learner achievement, 30–32, 121–122
Learning conversations, 152–155
Learning organizations, 152
Learning styles, 102–108
Legalized oppression, 79–80
Lifelong learning, 164
Lindsey, D. B., 28, 42, 81
Lindsey, R. B., xvii, 17, 28, 69, 70
Loewen, J. W., 80, 81
Lucas, T. see Senge, P.
Lutkus, A. D., 31

Macroaggressions, 65
Mainstream culture, 63
Maple View case study
    academic performance, 163
    adaptability, 148, 149
    background information, 19–24
    change processes, 145–146, 149
    collaboration, 126
    conflict management, 132, 133, 137–138
    cultural assessment, 103–104, 105, 110
    cultural blindness, 89
    cultural competence, 95–96
    cultural destructiveness, 81–82
    cultural incapacity, 85–86
    cultural knowledge, 160, 162

cultural precompetence, 91–93
cultural proficiency, 76–78
differences and similarities, 127–128, 129, 130
diversity-valuing behaviors, 117, 120–121, 124
educational impact, 168
institutional barriers, 70–71
instructional strategies, 106
negative judgments, 127–128
organizational culture, 112–113, 114
performance measures, 41
resistance to change, 59–60
respectfulness, 123, 124
teachable moments, 150
Marginalized students, 2
Marzano, R. J., 31, 34
McAllister, G., 134
McIntyre, A. M., 182
McParland, J., 180
Melting pot metaphor, 87
Method-based conflicts, 136, 139
Microaggressions, 15, 52–53, 64–65
Minority groups, 66
Mithun, J., 66
Modern racism, 80
Mood, A. M., 180
Moran, R., 31
Moss, A. A., Jr., 81
Multicultural resources, 32–34
Multicultural transformation, 12–13
Murray, C. B., 182
Myatt, K. *see* Lindsey, R. B.
Myrdal, G., 66

Naisbitt, J., 182
National Study Group for the Affirmative Development of Academic Ability, 30
Negative judgments, 127–128
Nelson, B., 27, 32
Nieto, S., 34
No Child Left Behind Act (2001), 26, 27, 30
Noddings, N., 25
Noguera, P., 70
Nuri-Robins, K., xvii, 17, 69, 70

Oakes, J., 31
Obama, B., ix–x
Ogbu, J., 66, 81
Oppressed immigrant groups, 66, 69
Oppressive systems, 59, 66–67, 79–81
Orfield, G., ix
Organizational change, 61–62
Organizational culture assessment, 111–114, 162–165

Outside involvement barriers, 72, 75
Owens, R. G., 182

Pahl, J. V. N. C., 28
Palmer, P. J., xxvi, 2, 167, 169
Pappano, L., 27
Parental involvement, 47–48, 53–55
Pearl, A., ix
Peercy, M. *see* Buendia, E.
Perceptions, 135–136, 139
Perie, M., 31
Perini, M. J., 183
Personal action plan, 169–179
Personality styles, 136, 139
Perspectives on education in America: Hearing before Subcommittee on Elementary, Secondary, and Vocational Education, Committee on Education and Labor, House of Representatives, 183
Peterson, B., 180
Pickering, D. J., 31, 34
Plessy v. Ferguson (1896), x
Politcally correct behavior, 15
Pollock, J. F., 31, 34
Popham, J. W., 28
Power, 151–152
Powers, J. M., 183
Practice, 16
Praxis, 16, 57, 157–158, 167–168
Precompetence, cultural, 5, 90–94, 98, 99
Principle of intentionality, 118–122, 146, 152, 169–170
Privileges, 63
Professional development, xxiii–xxvii, 31, 34
Public Schools Accountability Act (1999), 26

Racism, 80
Ravitch, D., 31
Reconstruction process, 166
Reeves, D. B., 163
Reflection, 16
Reflective practices
academic performance, 164
achievement standards, 37
adaptability, 148, 149, 151
beliefs and assumptions, 60–61
change processes, 62, 147, 149
collaboration, 127, 143
communities of practice, 158, 168
conflict management, 134–135, 140, 143
cultural assessment, 115
cultural competence, 56–57, 96–97
cultural destructiveness, 81–83
cultural diversity, 50

cultural identity, 45
cultural incapacity, 83–87
cultural knowledge, 161, 163
culturally defined needs, 51–52
cultural precompetence, 92–94
cultural proficiency, 98
differences and similarities, 129–130
diverse thought patterns, 55–56
diversity, 118
diversity-valuing behaviors, 119–120,
    125, 130, 172–173
dominant cultures, 46–49, 63, 68
educational impact, 168
hidden curriculum, 34
individual cultural assessment, 109–110,
    111, 170–171
influential instructors, 41–42
inner curriculum, 37
institutional barriers, 75
instructional planning, 29
instructional strategies, 167
learner performance, 121–122
learning styles, 104, 107–108
microaggressions, 52–53, 65
negative judgments, 128
oppressive systems, 67
organizational cultural assessment,
    112, 113–114, 164–165
parental involvement, 48, 54–55
praxis, 57
professional development, xxiv, 31
respectfulness, 123–124
scapegoats, 151–152
social encounter experiences, 12
standards, 30
targets and agents, 64
teachable moments, 151
value systems, 43, 44, 57
Resistance to change, 5, 58–59, 61–62
Resource barriers, 72, 74–75
Respect, 51, 122–125
Reyes, P., 34
Riehl, C. J., 134
Rist, R., 66
Roberts, C., 152
Rosenholtz, S. J., xxvi
Ross, R. B., 152
Roth, G., 152

Santamaria, L. J., 183
Satir, V., 183
Savage, T. V., 26, 27, 32, 33
Scapegoats, 151–152
Schein, E., 135, 163

Schneider, B., 33
Schoolcentric, 53
Scribner, A. P., 34
Scribner, J. D., 34
Senge, P., 152
Sennett, F., 2, 19, 25, 40, 58, 76, 102,
    116, 144, 159, 167
Sense of entitlement, 6
Sergiovanni, T. J., 183
Silver, H. F., 183
Sims, M. J., 27, 32
Singham, M., 70
Single-loop learning, 161
Sleeter, C. E, 29
Smith, B. S., 152
Sommers, W. L., 181
Standards
    achievement standards, 30–31
    definition, 16
    reform efforts, 26–29
    standards-based instruction,
        26–29, 32–35
    standards documents, 34–35
Stereotypes, 50, 64, 69–70
Strong, R. W., 183
Subject-based instruction, 27, 28–29
Sue, D. W., xviii, 52, 65
Systemic oppression, 5–6

Takaki, R., 81
Targets/target groups, 63–64
Teachable moments, 150–151, 164
Teaching philosophy, 40–41
Terminology, 14–17
Terrell, R. D., xvii, 17, 69, 70
Thomas, K., 142
Thompson, G. L., 32
Thought patterns, 55–56
Thousand, J. S., 33, 34
Tokenism, 83
Tolerance, 15
Tomlinson, C. A., 184

Ury, W., 135
U.S. Department of Education, ix

Value systems
    collaboration, 125–127
    conflict sources, 135, 139
    cultural assessment, 43–44, 57
    differences and similarities,
        116–118, 127–130
    intentionality, 118–122
    respectfulness, 122–125

Valuing diversity *see* Diversity-valuing behaviors
Vigil, J. D., 81
Villa, R. A., 33, 34
Voltz, D. L., 27, 32
Vygotsky, L. S., 76

Weinfeld, F. D., 180
Wellman, B., 181

Wenger, E., 157
Wheatley, M. J., 152
Wiggins, G. P., 33, 102
*Williams, Eliezer, et al. v. State of
    California et al.* (2004), 31
Wilmore, E. L., 27

York, R. L., 180

CORWIN
A SAGE Company

The Corwin logo—a raven striding across an open book—represents the union of courage and learning. Corwin is committed to improving education for all learners by publishing books and other professional development resources for those serving the field of PreK–12 education. By providing practical, hands-on materials, Corwin continues to carry out the promise of its motto: **"Helping Educators Do Their Work Better."**